Shouting *into*

*"I have never read anything like this! Shouting into the Silence
will take you on an incredible journey with Danny, as he quite
literally fights for the rights of other human beings across the
world. Looking at some famous cases and some lesser-known tales
you won't be able to put this moving and shocking book down.
Shouting into the Silence inspired me and it will inspire you
– a must read."*

Marc Carey, European Marketing Director, Hard Rock

*"This is an amazing book, telling the most riveting
stories of many people from all walks of life, who are passionate
about human justice and who work tirelessly to achieve it.
It is beautifully and sensitively told by Danny Smith, whose
determination 'to set the prisoner free' has never wavered. No
one can read this book and remain unmoved. With humility and
admiration, I salute you Danny."*

Fiona Castle OBE, Author and Broadcaster

*"If you ever doubt that one person can make a difference to the
world you should read this book. It reminded me that if you act
with courage, are driven by belief in justice and a big and kind
heart, you can be the change you want to see in the world. Danny
Smith's story is an inspiration and this book is a must read for a
new generation of activists."*

**Christopher Davis, Director of International Campaigns and
Corporate Social Responsibility, The Body Shop International;
United Nations Business Leaders Award January 2011**

Shouting
into the
Silence

One man's fight for the world's forgotten

DANNY SMITH

LION

Published by Lion Books
an imprint of
Lion Hudson plc
Wilkinson House, Jordan Hill Road,
Oxford OX2 8DR, England
www.lionhudson.com/lion

ISBN 978 0 7459 5600 8
e-ISBN 978 0 7459 5726 5

First edition 2013

Cover image © Charlie Barnwell/Corbis

Text acknowledgments
Every effort has been made to trace the original copyright holders where
required. In some cases this has proved impossible. We shall be happy to
correct any such omissions in future editions.

Editorial note
Some names in this book have been change to protect identities.

A catalogue record for this book is available from the British Library

Printed and bound in the UK, July 2013, LH26

To
Jessica –
the world changed the day you entered my life.

· ·

To
Joan,
Rachel, Matt, Seth, and Eden
Luke, Holly, and Lily –
you remind me of the important things in life.

Contents

Acknowledgments

I owe so much to so many – people who inspired me, worked with me, supported me, stood with me when things got rough, loved me...

Father Shay Cullen, Reverend KK Devaraj, Petru Dugulescu, Valeri Barinov, Alexander Ogorodnikov, Shoba and Sandesh Kaddam, Timothy Chmykhalov, the Vashchenko family, Peter Sewakiryanga, Vincent Mugisha, Bob Fu, Chen Guangcheng, Yuan Weijing – you enriched my life beyond measure.

Lizzie and David Alton's commitment never faltered from the first day Bill Hampson asked David to get involved, and Jubilee Campaign's accomplishments within Parliament can be traced to his door. Early in the journey, Peter Benenson was my mentor, and George Verwer a true friend through the years.

The compassion of people has been humbling. I wish I could list everyone who responded to the campaigns and projects I raised. It's heartening to know that there's so much goodness in the world.

I'm grateful to Ali Hull, whose dogged persistence ensured we reached port safe; to Julie Frederick and Jessica Tinker for final manoeuvres; and to my son Luke for important contributions in navigating the changes in the manuscript.

Many of the exploits recorded here wouldn't have happened without our crack team including Ann Buwalda, Rosie Till, Richard Warnes, Howard Taylor, Ali Kimber-Bates, Kate Thomas, Emily Swain, Mark Rowland, Malcolm Grainge, Robert Day, Stephen Andrews, John Anderson, Wilfred Wong, Rachel Bader, Jennie Cain, Alice Diamond, Naomi Weeks.

Family, friends, and colleagues, only a few are mentioned: My mother always put me first, Clement Dameron, Pam, Melanie, Tim and the Macmarquis clan; Janet and Craig Rickards, Wanno Haneveld, Roley Horowitz, Dr Wai Sin Hu, Hazel Thompson, Bill Hampson, Bernadette Charehwa and Ronald Mazengera, Jim and Kitty Thompson, Olivia Harrison, Steve Brown, Billy Connolly, James Parry, Paul Diamond, Patricia Hitchcock, Reg Wright, Steve Neill, Bonnie Ryason, Dave Muir, John Quanrad, Peter Kirtley, Liane Carroll, Bryce Cooke, Frank and Marlene Rice, Lois Brown, Rajiv Hanspal, Vinoth Kumar, Chris and Linda Denne, Christine Lock, Dave and Mathilda Armstrong, Ron and Lilo Penny, Fred and Helen Holmes, Andrew Smith, Alan Clemence, Sue Tatum, Micha Jazz, Ian and Rosemary Andrews, Dirk Jan Groot, Gerald Coates, Aninha Capaldi, Brian Woods, Deborah Shipley, Kate Blewett, Sarah de Carvalho, Chris Rogers, Mal Whitely, Kirsty Jones, Dave Dorey; the Reverends Ben and Chris Beecroft and members (both past and present) of St Paul's Church Addlestone embraced us at the toughest time of our lives – you will always have a special place in my heart.

Joan; Rachel, Matt, Seth, and Eden; Luke, Holly, and Lily; and Jessica... I love you.

Foreword

As a teenager I felt especially challenged by the killing of Dr Martin Luther King. King warned of the danger of silence in the face of the evil of prejudice and bigotry, and he made a passionate case in defence of liberty and of life itself. King warned that "our lives begin to end the day we become silent about things that matter" and that "in the end, we will remember not the words of our enemies but the silence of our friends."

Danny Smith could never be accused of silence or complacency when faced by the things which matter and no-one will ever be able to say of him that he was a fair-weather friend, with nothing to say and nowhere to be seen, when the going got rough. Anyone reading the gripping and inspiring stories in *Shouting into the Silence* will be struck by his selfless and sacrificial devotion to those to whom he has dedicated his life.

They will also be struck by his refusal to be deterred by seemingly impossible odds or daunted by the scale of the battles in which he has become involved.

Just over a decade after King was murdered, and now serving as a young MP at Westminster, to remind myself of the importance of doing what you can to make a difference – I pinned the words of King to my office wall in the House of Commons.

And it was here in Parliament, not long after, that I met Danny Smith and we discussed the plight of the Siberian Seven – whose story is in this book. It was the beginning of a fruitful partnership, which helped me crystallise my own thinking on the indissoluble links between human life, human rights and human dignity.

Dietrich Bonhoeffer, who was executed by the Nazis, also knew the other consequence of remaining silent – "Silence in the face of evil is itself evil: God will not hold us guiltless. Not to speak is to speak. Not to act is to act."

Danny Smith has spent three decades speaking and acting, shouting into the silence. This book will inspire another generation to do likewise.

David Alton
(Professor the Lord Alton of Liverpool)

Introduction

I pressed my hand against the window of Apple's flagship shop just off Oxford Street in London. My fingerprints left a faint outline on the cold luminous glass as I peered inside.

The Apple Store was teeming with people, and there was a buzz in the crowd. It seemed that everyone wanted an iPhone or an iPad or one of their cool, iconic products that had turned Apple into the world's most valuable company ever, setting a record $623 (£395) billion for its shares in August 2012.

I scoured the customers inside but couldn't see her. Hazel Thompson, the dynamic young contract photographer from *The New York Times*, had sounded urgent on the phone. "Can you meet me at Apple immediately?" I was intrigued.

* * *

Some months earlier, we had talked about the explosion of Twitter and Facebook and discussed how new media could be wielded to help children at risk. I always believed in using the media and our campaigns had been featured on television, radio, and the front pages of the biggest selling newspapers in the country. But times were changing. Tablets like Amazon's Kindle had become best sellers and electronic books were outselling fiction hardbacks and paperbacks. Apple's iTunes site was responsible for nearly 30 per cent of all music sold worldwide. By October 2012, Apple had reportedly sold 100 million iPads and expected the same number to be sold in 2013. The US's second largest selling news magazine, *Newsweek*, had decided its December 2012 issue would become its final print edition, closing to concentrate on its online edition. An editorial in *The Guardian* newspaper in January 2013 called the end of print a digital mass extinction and compared it with the disappearance of the dinosaurs millions of years ago.

"I've got some ideas," Hazel had said, eyes twinkling. "Wouldn't it be amazing if we could do an iBook and get Apple involved?"

I smiled at Hazel but stayed silent. It would be amazing. It was also most unlikely. Apple's genius was to create must-have products and everyone wanted to link up with them. Why would they get involved with us? Besides, they had never done anything like this before.

"I'll call you," Hazel said.

Hazel covered the London Olympics for ABC TV News (a US television station), and when the Games was over, she telephoned. She sounded both mysterious and excited. She wouldn't say much on the phone, just that it was an important meeting and I had to be there.

* * *

Over the past four decades, I have walked the streets of some of planet earth's mega cities, from Manila to Moscow to Mumbai. While media pundits documented global conflicts directed by madmen, bandits, freedom-fighters, rebels, tyrants, and terrorists, I have detected another battle in this geography of disgrace, hidden from view, moving invisibly but spreading fast: a war against children.

Tortured. Trafficked. Exploited. Prostituted. Enslaved. Starved. Burnt. Maimed. Sacrificed. Abused. Forced to work. Compelled into violent conflicts. Murdered... This has become the terrifying experience of millions of children worldwide. Across the globe it is the children – those who are vulnerable and in need of our care – who are most at risk.

My journey into this "war zone" has led me to some extraordinary people – warriors who inspired me and joined me in campaigning to protect children at risk. As the founder of Jubilee

Campaign, combining lobbying and transformational charitable action, I think my role has been easy. I was both a witness of the injustice children faced and a designer – I designed ways for people to make a difference. The response has been humbling. Friends, neighbours, supporters, politicians, journalists – people from all walks of life took a part; many sent sacrificial gifts, some gave generously and asked nothing in return, including George and Olivia Harrison, and Billy Connolly. Princess Diana sent us a personal message and we'd heard that she planned to get more involved before her untimely death in a car crash in 1997.

It's been an unforgettable journey, with some chilling moments, such as that memorable night in Epsom, when I stripped off for my first undercover assignment.

CHAPTER 1

Wired for Sound

Trying to Change the Law on Sex Tourism, 1994

It was late in the evening and Epsom's multi-storey car park was deserted. We drove in a convoy up to the third level and pulled over into one of the empty bays. Fast Eddie was the first out and ambled over, carrying a heavy silver case.

"OK, this is it," he said. "Take off your clothes."

I took off my shirt and pulled down my trousers. Goosebumps came up on my body as I felt the cool evening breeze.

The squeal of tyres startled us. A black Golf GTI came into view. It hit the curve of the exit route and cruised by. We froze for an instant and must have had the collective look of a fawn caught in the brights of a car's main beam. The driver of the Golf seemed to be a prim, no-nonsense career woman. You could read her quizzical expression as she took in the scene, setting her mental clock to be sure to catch *Crimewatch* the following Tuesday. "Yes, officer, there were six of them. They looked really mean. One was stripped, almost naked."

"Come on guys, let's get to work." It was Fast Eddie, and in the next twenty minutes we realized how he had earned his nickname.

Fast Eddie pulled open the silver case to reveal a cascade of electronic gadgetry. His blonde assistant, Jade, strapped a miniature tape recorder to my lower chest and a sound box to my side. I pulled on my shirt and a loose-fitting jacket that I had bought for £1 from

Oxfam earlier that day. They traced the wires through my clothes and plugged me in. Jade checked sound levels. At first, it was hard to breathe with the multi-flex heavy-duty tape cutting into my skin and the equipment strapped so tightly to my body. Adam Chadwick, who was in charge of the operation, pointed to my reflection in the car mirror. "You've put on a lot of weight," he smirked.

Meanwhile Fast Eddie was putting the final touches to something in the high-tech gizmo from his bag of tricks. It was a necktie. Attached to it were wires linked to a sleek-looking box with flashing lights. He carefully eased the tie over my head and placed it around my neck. Jade traced the cable through my shirt and plugged it into the sound box taped to my waist.

"OK, we're live," Fast Eddie announced. He twiddled with some buttons and static burst out from the sound box. "Let's hit it."

With deft, precise strokes, they wired me for sound and pictures. A low light flicked from the small television monitor that Jade was holding and Adam's image appeared on the screen. Adam stood in front of me and waved. And there he was on the monitor, waving. But where was the image coming from? Jade pointed to my necktie.

The tie wasn't going to win any design awards. Little diamond-shaped motifs the size of a tiny button were set tight against a silvery silk material. At the centre of the pattern of one of the diamond shapes was a tiny camera lens.

Fast Eddie's work was immaculate. The camera was virtually undetectable and the floppy coat covered the recorders taped to my body. He was in constant demand by television journalists and had worked on many undercover investigations. Adam had chosen this particular day for our operation because he wanted Fast Eddie for the job. He told me, "It's going to be dangerous and I want to be sure we have the best."

"You know what you have to do, don't you?" Fast Eddie said, talking me through the best positions to capture the target on the secret camera.

* * *

In November 1994, a producer at Independent Television News (ITN) wrote and asked if they could join us on an undercover operation that we had started, investigating travel agents in the UK who were selling "child sex" tours overseas.

Since 1992, Jubilee Campaign had been at the forefront of a battle to change the law so that sex tourists who abused children around the world could be prosecuted when they got back to the UK. We worked in partnership with Father Shay Cullen, an Irish Catholic priest from the Columban missionary order in the Philippines, who was the first to call for this new legislation.

Father Shay and his organization, the Preda Foundation, had spent several years investigating sex offenders, and his own files rivalled those of the authorities. Shay passed us a list of suspects and offenders while we were researching material for a report into child prostitution that we intended to publish as part of our campaign to convince the government to change the law.

Under existing legislation, men could videotape themselves violating children overseas but if they were caught at Heathrow Airport on their return to the UK, they could only be prosecuted for carrying obscene videos. The sex acts against children were not punishable. It was absurd.

I woke up in a sweat one night while working on the material that Shay had sent over, worried that people on the list could sue us. I telephoned Shay immediately, and sounded the alarm.

"We could end up in court," I said, clearly panicked.

"Great," Shay thundered down a crackly line from the Philippines. "Can you imagine the scene? You're in court and the paedophile offender is suing you for exposing him?"

"But he could file a case against us," I countered.

"Don't worry if you get sued, I'll raise the money for your bail!" Shay chuckled.

He calmed me down. "Keep your nerve," he counselled. It was a dangerous strategy but the right one.

Soon after this, I had an appointment with an MP to seek his support for our campaign. As I was waiting in the hallway of an anteroom in the House of Commons one rainy afternoon, I picked up a leaflet that had been dropped by the occupants of an earlier session. It revealed that a group of jazz enthusiasts met regularly in Parliament. At first it was funny. I imagined a smoky room late at night, filled with MPs and their cohorts bopping to the rhythms that came off the riverboats that sailed up the Mississippi through New Orleans and Memphis, with the beat carried over on the slave ships from Africa. After the amusement had passed, I became inquisitive. If jazz fans met regularly in the Commons, could we have a parliamentary group dedicated to street children?

There were some immediate hurdles to overcome. Who would handle the administrative backup? Problem solved: Jubilee Campaign would serve as its secretariat. How could we choose a chairman without displaying any political bias? Easy, we'd have three.

David Alton, at the time the Liberal MP for Liverpool, eased the passage for the formation of the group, and recruited Nigel Griffiths (Labour) and Ian Bruce (Conservative) as co-chairmen with him. Olivia Harrison, the wife of former Beatle George Harrison, and Jim Capaldi's Brazilian wife Aninha, invited their friends Jimmy Nail, Wimbledon Football Club chairman Sam Hammam, among others, and the All Party Parliamentary Group on Street Children (APPGSC) was launched in the House of Commons later that year, dedicated to using the political system to defend the rights of vulnerable children on the streets. If the parliamentary group thought they wouldn't have much to do, they were wrong.

The new APPGSC's first meeting was in November to launch our campaign to change the law to prosecute sex tourists who abused children overseas. The materials in our campaign toolkit included a petition to the government, postcards to local MPs, and the 132-page report that I'd been working on with Shay. He flew over for the event at a packed room in the House of Commons.

Our message was clear: we wanted child prostitution outlawed, declared a crime against humanity, and extra-territorial jurisdiction legislation introduced for sex crimes against children. At the time, no foreign government or Western nation had ever arrested any of its citizens who had abused children overseas and there was simply no mechanism in place to prosecute offenders.

The statistics proved sobering for everyone at the meeting. Every year, about 1 million children were lured or forced into prostitution. This figure was documented in a Norwegian government report, confirming that young children were trafficked and held as bait for a thriving attraction: sex with children.

Globally, as many as 10 million children were thought to be enslaved in the sex industry, prostitution and pornography. Child prostitution tended to be higher in Asia and Latin America, although an alarming growth rate had been recorded in Africa, North America, and Europe. Eastern Europe and the former communist states were emerging as a new market in the sexual exploitation of children.

The UN Rapporteur on Child Trafficking remarked that the children being tricked into prostitution were getting younger and younger. "These are nine-, ten-, eleven-, twelve-year-old kids," he asserted. The experts warned that the trend would increase unless action was taken.

Shay combined eloquence with clarity at the parliamentary meeting as he outlined the historical context from which to view this crime: "Sex tourism and child prostitution is the ultimate in exploitation. Peoples of other nations have exploited the raw materials of poorer countries for centuries. Now they're coming back to exploit the bodies of our children."

Our campaign emphasized that the authorities had failed to bring paedophiles to justice. Instead, these sex tourists had used the system to evade capture, putting more children at risk. It was time for a new law.

Several television journalists attended the meeting and later a documentary was commissioned. Hundreds of copies of our report were sent to MPs, the police, the press, and others. But the government's initial response wasn't encouraging.

At a meeting led by MPs from the APPGSC, the Home Office said that the problem was too complex and the law couldn't be changed to accommodate our demands. It would never happen. Their explanation was that such laws would be unworkable in practice because of the difficulties in gathering evidence from foreign jurisdictions to facilitate a successful prosecution. The Home Office insisted that it was not for the British government to impose its laws abroad. That was that. To strengthen our efforts we joined ECPAT (End Child Prostitution and Asian Tourism) but continued several independent initiatives over the next few years.

In 1994, our parliamentary officer, Wilfred Wong, drafted a bill setting out the laws we sought and put a requirement of double criminality in the proposed legislation. This meant that the alleged child sex offence had to be considered as a criminal offence both in the foreign territory where it occurred and within the UK before the accused could be charged and prosecuted in this country. He explained:

> *I did this because there was no way the British government would agree to imposing its laws on another jurisdiction if the crime in question was not even considered an offence in that foreign jurisdiction.*
>
> *Furthermore, I put in the requirement that nothing in the bill would contravene the legal principle of Double Jeopardy. This meant that if the defendant had already been prosecuted and either convicted or acquitted for the offence while abroad, he could not be prosecuted for the same offence again when he returned to Britain.*

We used every opportunity to lobby the government. They expressed sympathy but performed the ceremony of the folded arms. They would do everything they could but there was nothing they could do. Britain once led the world in ending the slave trade, but by the early nineties, it became one of the only major tourist-sending countries (alongside Japan) to refuse to introduce a law prosecuting its own nationals for exploiting children overseas.

The government's feeble excuses effectively left them on the side of the sex tourists. It was hard to understand why more was not being done to protect children at risk. How could we allow children around the world to be enslaved and held captive for adults to jet in and defile them? How would history judge us? I was determined we should do everything possible to fight this.

Getting my hands dirty

I was sure that the fast track to the government's attention was to get the story into the press. When Father Shay showed me the videotape of the arrest of a suspected paedophile – a foreigner – on a boat with young children (some aged seven) in the Philippines, I was convinced that the story would cause a sensation. After screening the video, the media groups we approached were enthusiastic, but when they learned that the suspect, Victor Fitzgerald, was Australian and not British, the decision was swift and emphatic: the offender had to be British or the story wouldn't run. But Father Shay continued to work closely with us on new investigations into the dark, sordid, claustrophobic world of sex tourists and several leads emerged. With the backing of ITN, we knew the story had legs.

But it also meant I had to get involved, get my hands dirty. ITN wanted me to focus on a specific target: Mike Stones, the boss of a Surrey travel agency called 747 Travel. When I phoned him to make contact in November 1994, he talked enthusiastically about the sex industry abroad and promised personally to escort me around the bars and brothels of Thailand and the Philippines – after I had bought a ticket from him, of course.

"We can get you anything you want," Stones said convincingly, "including young girls."

"How young?" I asked.

He replied, "Just tell me how young you want the girls. Just give me an age. Give me a number. No problem at all. You can do anything you want with the kids."

He wanted a cheque in the post for my ticket but I insisted that we meet, and the lure of my payment proved too enticing. I had tape-recorded a few of our telephone conversations but I needed his words on camera, if the story were to run on television.

We were clear that there could be no entrapment or manipulation or the story would be discredited and open the door for us to be sued. All I had to do was ask the questions. All the suspect had to do was repeat his everyday conversation – on camera. The risks were obvious. If Stones suspected that I had been filming him secretly or that he'd been exposed, he'd probably erupt in fury and turn violent. Worse, the investigation would be jeopardized and he would escape and be able to cover his tracks.

When ITN learned that Stones worked from home and sold his sex tours within a mile of Chessington's World of Adventures, they had the hook for an important story.

* * *

I liked James Dean and Marlon Brando and harboured secret dreams of becoming an actor, but playing the role of a paedophile soliciting children for sex was one of the toughest things I've ever had to do. I would give my life for my children, who were safe at home, given all the love and care that our hearts could afford. But here I was, late at night, in leafy, tranquil Surrey, about to meet a sleaze bag who had already told me that he had sold airline tickets to perverts so they could travel abroad to abuse children.

From the car park in Epsom we drove the short journey to 747 Travel, situated in an elegant suburb near Epsom Station. The film crew set up their equipment in the bushes at the side of the road and focused their camera on Stones's front door.

I walked down the quiet avenue and pressed the doorbell. I was sweating, both from nervous tension and the equipment strapped to my body. The tape cut into my flesh and the decks and the wires under my clothes felt uncomfortable. Curiously, I felt a sense of calm, despite my obvious anxiety.

Somewhere to the left, I caught a glimpse of a woman being pulled along by a dog straining on its leash. In the distance, a car engine started up, followed quickly by the crackle-crunch of tyres on gravel. The door opened and I walked inside.

CHAPTER 2

Undercover

*Campaign Against Child Sex Gathers Momentum,
1994–95*

I closed the door behind me and followed Stones inside. He walked in short, jerky steps. He looked to be in his late thirties, thickset, with tousled hair and glasses. He wore trainers and dressed casually.

The next forty minutes were excruciating as he went into explicit details of his sordid business of sex tours. Stones made it clear that my apparent interest in young girls wasn't unusual: anything that I wanted was easily available, and he knew where to get it.

It was almost over. We walked back to the front door. He slouched forward as he turned the latch and opened it. It was dark outside and there was a dampness in the air. The glow from a street lamp shone into the hallway where we were standing and cast long shadows down the passage. Somehow I had to get over these final moments together, get past him, out of this place. But he had blocked the door.

I could feel a fresh breeze blow gently into the hallway where we stood. The equipment under my clothes felt heavy and clumsy. Stones was staring at me. Could he see something? A wire sticking out of my collar at the back? A lead dangling from my trouser pocket? Bumps under my shirt?

For the first time during the encounter, I felt tense, apprehensive that he would uncover the secret recording device strapped to my body and the hidden camera in my tie. If he did, I thought that he might attack me, and it felt curiously exciting. Secretly, I hoped he'd hit me. I wanted him to grab the secret camera and shout at me. Then I could strike him down. Within a few seconds, a great anger had welled up inside.

During my visit, Stones had confirmed that he could arrange my "sex tour". He would lead me by the hand and take me to places of perverted sex. He would take me himself. I could indulge repeatedly with impunity during my holiday. There would be no limits, and no concerns from any authorities, should they see an adult man and a child. Stones would do this for me. He did this for all his clients. This was his service, his personal service. He was proud of his credentials, his in-country network.

Could I take him? I tried to recall the boxing moves of people such as Sonny Liston and Mike Tyson. Should I defend myself or go on the attack?

It happened fast. Stones reached out and touched my arm.

"Don't worry," he said reassuringly. "We'll sort you out."

He assumed that I was anxious about the trip and I had to convince him that he was right. I decided to go after one final offensive to get him to speak directly to my tie. "But what if I can't find the girls or they're not that young?" I said, trying to keep my voice steady, detached from the anger that I was really feeling.

"I've told you. That's not a problem. Just tell me how young you want the girls," he said, in a matter-of-fact tone. "I can set this up. Just let me have the dates when you can go."

We shook hands and he stepped aside. He remarked on the cool breeze and thought the evenings were getting darker. He hoped for good weather, a light winter.

I walked out of the house and into the night. All I could hear were my footsteps on the pavement, out of time with the rattle of recorders and cameras. I was no longer worried about wires and connections, the pictures that my tie would capture or the sound quality being ruptured by the rustling of my clothes. I just wanted to get away.

On the trail

Fast Eddie gave me a hug. "You did good."

Adam Chadwick was tense. He looked sternly at me. "You were in there too long. We were worried. You shouldn't have stayed that long."

"But there was nothing I could do," I protested. "He was on the phone to a client. I had to wait."

"We were coming in to get you," Adam replied.

We drove to a pub in Epsom and, in the darkness of the car park, they took me apart. The equipment was unplugged and replaced in the silver case, the masking tape gently ripped from my body. It stung. Fast Eddie played the tape on the portable television. Stones's face stared back at me, askance at times, but he was on camera. There was relief all round. I knew I could convince him to talk to me but didn't know if I could manage the technology. There had been a lot of instructions to remember. It was like getting into a car for the first time while someone gives you a crash course in driving – minutes before your test.

The next morning Adam phoned me at the office. He was pleased with the results but said that the picture focus on Stones had been erratic.

"What did you think of his friend?" Adam asked.

"What friend?" I replied.

"His friend who goes out to Thailand and the Philippines to pick up young girls."

I was puzzled. I couldn't recall anything like that.

"Well it's on the tapes," he confirmed. Adam gave me a summary of my conversation with Stones. When I had expressed apparent concern over trying to find young girls on my own, Stones had reassured me that he could get the job done. Why, he had done it many times before, and my interests coincided with those of a friend of his. Peter knew his way around. And if I was worried, I could accompany them. I had no recollection of Stones referring to anyone else.

"Who is this mystery man?" I wondered.

All we had on the tape was a name: Peter. The tapes disclosed that Peter went out regularly four times a year: Christmas, Easter, summer, autumn. Adam speculated that he might be a teacher in a school or college. "It fits with school terms," he mused.

After listening to the taped conversation, Adam was convinced that our investigation would result in an effective campaign to protect vulnerable children from such people. Our repulsion was tinged with rage but we knew it would accomplish very little. It had to be turned to strengthen our campaign. We needed information about his friend Peter. I dialled 747 Travel's number, and switched on the tape recorder.

It was a long call. Every few minutes, Stones put me on hold while he dealt with enquiries; when it was a customer booking a trip, he'd ask me to call back. I did.

We had developed a rapport and chatted easily. My acting skills had been enhanced as I forced myself to be convincing as a potential "difficult" customer seeking reassurance. It worked. I had a surname. I scribbled it down on a sheet of paper in front of me. Now I wanted to get out. Stones pressed me on dates. He mentioned a few.

"I'll get back to you," I said.

I hung up the phone and dialled Adam at the television company and gave him the information. Over the next few days, we learned a lot about Stones's friend. He'd been traced to a block of flats in Sutton where he lived with his mother. His telephone number was ex-directory. He didn't have a police record, but he did have a van that he rented out. He was a lecturer and his college had been identified. It was in London. And we had a surname – Mitchell.

We had to go after him. But how could we make contact? Rent the van? Bump into him in the college? In the street? ITN wanted me to invite Stones and Mitchell to a meal in a particular restaurant where the table would be rigged with a hidden camera and recorder. But this was dropped. It was risky and unpredictable.

There was no option. I would have to go back to Stones.

We were concerned that he'd become annoyed at the time being wasted so I did as he requested. I came up with some dates. But this was conditional. I was spending a lot of money. I wanted reassurance that this was going to be worth it. Reassurance from someone who had done this before. I wanted reassurance from his friend, Peter Mitchell, in person. It took some haggling but eventually Stones agreed to talk to Mitchell.

"I can't be sure he'll do it but we're meeting for a drink at the weekend and I'll ask him if he'll meet you," Stones said, struggling to contain his irritation. "Call me on Monday."

It worked. Mitchell said he'd call me. Probably. He would call on Thursday evening.

The television company parked me in a room near their studios on Euston Road but they raised the stakes. It wasn't enough to get him on the phone. We had to get him on camera. We had to meet.

The room was part of an ITN office unit and it was crammed full of files and merchandising from old television programmes. There were two desks back to back and several phones but only one was plugged into a tape recorder. The first hour passed. It was important not to get distracted and to stay focused. "Lord!" I said aloud. I never felt a grip on my body or a touch on my hand resting on the telephone. But neither was I seized by panic. I was holding the pattern. Just about.

The second hour passed. It was getting late. He had forgotten. He had the wrong date. He had the wrong time. He had scribbled down the wrong number. He had left it in a shirt that was in the washing machine. Stones had lied to me. He'd never given Mitchell the message. Mitchell had lied to Stones. Yeah. Yeah. Yeah. He had no intention of making the call. Mitchell was enraged with Stones. You told him what? Why did you tell him about me? Who is he?

The phone rang.

It was Peter Mitchell. He was different from Stones. He was sharp, cautious, brusque, and not eager to talk. All he would admit to was using 747 Travel to get cheap flights. And, grudgingly, he agreed to help me if we met in some exotic location. Help me, if he could. There was nothing on the tape that connected him to anything that Stones had said. He was slick. The call had been a failure. Lord...

But just before the final click of the telephone, a glimmer. Unexpectedly, he agreed to meet. Well, maybe. Mitchell told me that he'd be in a pub in Epsom on Sunday night. If I wanted to buy him a pint, he wouldn't object.

"I'll be there around eight. I'll be there for about fifteen minutes."

He hung up.

* * *

On Sunday the crew and I met at three o'clock in the Pizza Hut restaurant on South Street in Epsom. Fast Eddie was on a job and Adam Holloway, an investigative journalist (and later a Conservative MP), took his place. He was in charge and we reviewed the information. He thought the story was developing well and would make *News at Ten*. The government would have to take notice. But the next few hours were decisive as we needed Mitchell to talk on camera without any hint of manoeuvring or entrapment from me. Adam wanted me to keep Mitchell talking outside the pub when we left, while facing the van with blacked-out windows so that they could get a clear shot of his face. The cameras would be rolling.

The team ordered pizza but I'd lost my appetite.

I stripped off my clothes in one of Epsom's many cul-de-sacs. It was dark and no one looked twice. They checked me for sound and pictures. Just before I reached my car to drive to the pub, Adam Holloway dashed over, ruffled my shirt, brushed me down quite forcefully, and then gave me a playful tap on my cheek. "You'll be fine," he said.

Mitchell was dead on time and easy to spot. A large hulking figure, he looked sweaty and unfriendly. He asked for Fosters and, when I returned with two pints, he directed me to the rear of the pub which was quieter. I'd told him that I'd be holding a copy of *The Sunday Times* and I placed the papers on the table in front of us.

Mitchell looked at the papers and said gruffly, "You're not from the press, are you?"

It was a shaky start but things got better. He declined my offer of a second pint but during our half hour together, he accepted my cover story. He told me that he was a frequent visitor and regularly used 747 Travel's cheap fares, once for a long weekend, because the tickets were so inexpensive. Mitchell showed me pictures of a hotel that he part-owned. But he wasn't a property tycoon; he was a sex tourist. Though he talked guardedly, his own words provided confirmation.

As we stepped out of the pub, I asked him what car he drove, and we lingered on the steps discussing vehicles while facing the nondescript van with blacked-out windows. The ordeal was over. Mitchell got in his black Ford and drove off in the direction of Stones's house. He never noticed a motorbike take off at the same time, set well back.

The next day Adam Chadwick told me that I had done well by sticking to the script and no one could accuse us of entrapment. However, there was a problem. The camera hadn't picked up any pictures but they could still use the piece because the sound quality was good. They had footage of Mitchell outside the pub and intended to film Stones and Mitchell together when we confirmed the booking. The intention was to accompany them to Thailand before confronting them, and the trip was scheduled for late December. It was difficult to contemplate being away from the family at Christmas, especially on such an assignment, but it was equally hard to think that Stones, Mitchell, and their crowd would be in a faraway land, abusing children, possibly even on Christmas Day.

Then the TV people pulled out of the Christmas trip and told me they would pick up the story in the New Year. It was frustrating to hear that the story was on hold, knowing so much about their activities and powerless to stop them. Little did I know that another sex-tour operator, Michael Clarke of Paradise Express, would soon steal the spotlight.

Father Shay Cullen

In the eighties, I'd read an article about child prostitution by John Pilger in the *Daily Mirror* which revealed how he had purchased a child in Thailand. It haunted me. I had wanted to respond earlier, but we were a small organization and I didn't think anything we could do would make any difference.

All that changed the day I met Father Shay Cullen in 1992.

While attending a conference in the Philippines, I dropped out of some sessions to investigate the commercial sex industry. Even a cursory glance in the clubs and bars confirmed that children were ensnared, and while most charities had "projects", it seemed that all roads led to an Irish priest: he was the go-to man on the issue.

The people that I'd met up to that point talked of projects and programmes, how many could be helped, statistics that showed "bangs for your bucks". Father Shay was the first person who acted – and believed – that things could really change, and that we, as individuals, could do something to make it happen. It was an epiphany.

Shay patrolled the jails and the back streets of Olongapo City, once called the biggest brothel in the world. This was his parish. The street children and child prostitutes were his flock. His objective was to defend the rights of children, and he tracked down suspected paedophiles with the combined dedication of an Old Testament prophet and a modern-day detective.

In 1983, Shay had uncovered US Navy personnel who had abused children, some as young as nine years old. When this was exposed, Shay was shocked to discover two things: the US Navy were reluctant to help, and local Filipino politicians benefiting from the US trade pressured him to join the cover-up.

For more than nine decades, the United States had maintained a military presence among the 7,017 scattered islands that make up the Republic of the Philippines, with the biggest naval base outside America located at Subic Bay, and the US Air Force squadron situated at nearby Angeles City. While America was at war in Vietnam, the military used the Philippines for rest and recreation.

Shay's one-man campaign exposed the exploitation of children and women. He clashed repeatedly with corrupt local politicians and businessmen, who depended on the bars and brothels patronized by servicemen and tourists for the economic survival of the city. Harassment and intimidation gave way to deportation orders and death threats; the very officials who should have arrested the paedophiles and abusers were the ones trying to expel Shay.

Shay was practical and down to earth and he became a family friend, visiting us every time he came to the UK.

Manhunt in the Philippines

Adam Chadwick rang me at home one Saturday in February 1995 and said, "We need to talk. There have been some developments."

Adam was blunt. ITN had hooked up with a second organization who had recently started a similar investigation to ours into sex-tour operators. We would still be included as part of the story but the Stones/Mitchell investigation was on hold.

It was a blow. ITN had approached us and we had turned down other media to work exclusively with them. But a bigger concern was that Stones and Mitchell were fading into the distance. However, Adam didn't have time for a discussion.

ITN had assigned Adam Holloway, who had filmed my interview with Peter Mitchell, to investigate the story and he was focused on Paradise Express, a travel agency owned by Michael Clarke in Eastbourne. Clarke had advertised in *Exchange and Mart*, soliciting customers for an "Adult Disneyland" in the Philippines. Holloway videotaped Clarke in Eastbourne and he was captured on a hidden camera, promising young girls to potential customers. Soon after the covert recording, Holloway signed up with Paradise Express on a holiday to the Philippines, along with a representative from the second organization. ITN linked up with Shay and dates were confirmed.

It was tough watching "our story" get taken over, and worrying that ITN seemed to be stonewalling whenever the subject of Stones and Mitchell came up. My role had been diminished to that of a consultant, so I decided not to accompany ITN and the other organization as they set off with Michael Clarke to the Philippines.

Clarke unwittingly led Holloway through the sex industry in the Philippines, and ITN's secret filming was successful. The final scene was a confrontation on the beach, in which Holloway revealed he was not a sex tourist but an undercover reporter. With the television cameras still rolling, Clarke erupted, denied the charges, and stormed off.

ITN were wrapping up the story and, as they were completing the final edit, I asked Adam if he could include something about Stones and Mitchell. He said he'd try but didn't hold out much hope.

The story was broadcast on ITV News over two nights on 16 and 17 May 1995, with prominent coverage about Jubilee Campaign and an interview with me. This was the first time that a top news programme had linked the key components of the issue. The news report demonstrated how easy it was for British sex tourists to abuse children, and the impunity with which tour groups like Paradise Express operated.

The news report caused a little tremor around the UK. We received telephone calls and letters from people everywhere expressing support for our campaign to change the law in Britain. We urged them to write to Prime Minister John Major and to their local MP, and many did, sending us copies of their correspondence.

The advertising director of *Exchange and Mart* telephoned me and said he was sickened that his reputable publication had been exploited in this way. He told me he'd be fired if this was repeated and he asked for our help in monitoring the magazine's advertising content.

"We're concerned about something else in there," I said, and gave him the page number of Stones's advert in *Exchange and Mart*. Although not as sexually explicit as "Adult Disneyland", it was a nod and a wink.

The advertising director asked, "Do you have any evidence?"

"*We* don't." My frustration was carried in the exaggerated emphasis on the word "we". There was evidence. We didn't have it; ITN did. I called *News at Ten*'s office and asked if we could have the tapes, but "upstairs" wouldn't agree to pass them over. No explanation was given.

CNN in the Philippines had broadcast an edited version of ITV's news special and it rocked the country. The Paradise Express operation was in meltdown; Clarke had disappeared. A nationwide manhunt was announced: FIND MICHAEL CLARKE! But the police had no leads and the bars were covering their tracks. No one knew anything.

He had got away.

Hylton's Bill

At the time, Parliament was considering the Criminal Justice Bill and ECPAT persuaded Lord Archer of Sandwell, QC, a former solicitor general in the Labour Party, to table the bill that our parliamentary officer had drafted as an amendment to the Criminal Justice Bill. Conservative government opposition ensured its failure, but Lord Hylton, the independent crossbench peer, picked it up again in the House of Lords.

Our petition to change the law had been signed by over 20,000 people and, early in July 1995, Glenda Jackson MP delivered it to Downing Street, calling for government action. The Oscar-winning actress had been an MP for two years and gave another award-winning performance, capturing television and radio coverage for the campaign. But our enthusiasm wilted as, hours later that same day, the government let it be known through a Home Office announcement that it would oppose the passage of Hylton's bill in the Commons. Their compromise was to consider prosecuting sex-tour operators instead. Clearly someone had watched the ITV report. In parliamentary code, this was the bill's death knell. The government continued to insist that the bill was unworkable. However, that argument was decisively squashed when a Swedish court successfully prosecuted a 69-year-old former civil servant, Bengt Bolin, for sexual intercourse with a fourteen-year-old boy while on holiday in Thailand on 18 February 1993.

The British government was put under further pressure with the increasing media coverage. We didn't need to pump out much publicity. ITV had done the job for us. Several journalists called and asked to join us on a similar story. But these investigations were time-consuming, and we still had hopes of reviving the 747 Travel story with ITV.

* * *

A friend introduced me to Roger Insall, a senior reporter at the *News of the World*, and after an initial meeting at their Wapping office, he suggested that we link up. Although I had some reservations, I felt the risk was worth taking. Roger was a veteran investigative journalist and he worked for the newspaper with the largest circulation in Britain. If we wanted to get the attention of the politicians in Westminster, this opportunity offered us a megaphone.

Roger called a few days later and, as we reviewed things, three clear stories emerged. First, there was the Australian, Victor Fitzgerald, whose arrest Shay had videotaped. Second, Roger had located Michael Clarke's business partner in Paradise Express. Third, another target, whom he didn't identify, had links to a television soap star. "It's a long shot but I'm on the trail," he said, sounding mischievous.

The hint of a scandal linked to a celebrity was enough of a hook for the newspaper to turn up the heat. The *News of the World* wanted the story. And they wanted it now.

Roger said, "I'm leaving in two days. Are you in?"

CHAPTER 3

Investigation

On Location in the Philippines, 1995

It was a double whammy. Manila's fierce heat socked me hard and left me parched, while the humidity crept in like a sneaking fog, and drained any energy that was left. But the courtesy car from the airport had "air-con", and so the drive to the hotel was pleasant.

I knew the city's gigantic garbage dump had spawned a shanty town whose inhabitants scavenged from it, but noticed it had been cleared from the site. The cab driver explained, "It offended the tourists."

"What happened to the people?" The squatter camp had been well documented, showing the squalid life of families forced to survive from the remains of the city.

"Gone," he chuckled, gesticulating with his hand, a flicking movement to convey something hurtled into the oblivion of Manila's unknown.

We talked a little, or rather, he talked, and I nodded with regularity. I fitted the profile: a lone male, on an anonymous visit, mixing business with a holiday. It didn't take long: "If you want a nice friendly girl, I can fix it. I'm always at the hotel. Just tell reception that you want a car and ask for Frankie as your driver."

Frankie had simplified things and it was easy to see how quickly travellers could drift into sexual encounters. With poverty at epidemic levels, the pressure to deliver tourists' requests was heightened. The trade was driven by the demand. Frankie could fix anything I wanted. He'd done it before; he would do it again. It was a chilling welcome to Manila.

Roger Insall had flown in earlier, with the *News of the World* photographer Alastair Pullen, but they weren't in their room. I left a message for them at reception.

When I dialled Shay's number in Olongapo City, he was in the midst of an operation, talking fast, interrupting our conversation every few minutes to bark out messages to someone with him.

"Guess what?" Shay yelled over the phone. "Michael Clarke is hiding out here. The Paradise Express operation has blown up."

"Did the police trace him?"

"No," Shay replied. "I've just had a tip-off. But we've got to be careful or he'll pay off a corrupt policeman and get away."

Although Shay knew where Clarke was hiding, he was waiting for a policeman he knew so that the arrest wouldn't be bungled.

"He's going to be arrested tonight or tomorrow at dawn," Shay said. "How quickly can you get down to Olongapo?"

Not quickly enough.

While I was on the phone to Shay, Roger had called my room. They were at the bar. The news about Clarke was important. Roger needed a few stories with British links to ensure that the paper definitely ran his piece, but when we checked logistics, geography, and travel arrangements, it was clear that we couldn't make the two-hour journey to Olongapo in time.

When I phoned Shay back, he'd already left for the stake-out on Clarke, with officers he trusted from the National Bureau of Investigation (NBI).

Later that night, Shay confirmed that Clarke had been arrested. "They got him. He didn't get away. I think they're taking him back to Manila tonight or maybe early tomorrow morning."

On hearing the news, the three of us headed out to the NBI headquarters but no one knew anything about the arrest. Around midnight, Roger decided to scout out the clubs downtown in Makati and Ermita.

He'd been there before and knew his way around. There were foreigners in most of the bars, drinking with the girls, fooling around. The girls asked us to buy them drinks, so Roger pulled out a fistful of Filipino dollars, and everyone was a friend. Roger learned that the city had ostensibly been cleaned up in a recent crusade to outlaw prostitution, but in reality little had changed. The sex trade had been driven underground, into private houses and out of town.

In a backstreet dingy club an older woman asked if I was interested in any of the girls at the bar. I asked if there were any younger girls available. The woman wagged her finger in the air in a mock scolding motion and said there were many sixteen-year-old girls nearby, but she could have someone younger the next day. "I can bring you a girl who is about eleven or twelve years old, but you'll have to see her in the evening because she's still at school and can't stay out too late." The woman scribbled her name and phone number on a card and handed it to me.

The line had shifted with ease between women, teenagers, and younger girls and it wasn't difficult to understand that everyone wanted to please the customer, so everything became acceptable. I'd fought and lost a battle with jet lag so was relieved when Roger decided that he'd caught enough of Manila's low life for "background". It was a late night.

Shay arrived at our hotel the following morning and we headed off for the NBI offices to find Michael Clarke. We had to wait for some time at reception and positioned ourselves under the ceiling fan. Michael Clarke was inside one of the offices and, after waiting an hour, when the sentry outside the room was called away we slipped in to see him.

The dye in his hair had started to fade but he had showered, shaved, and, dressed in a grey striped suit, looked slim, slinky, and smart. He sat under a fan, like everyone else, trying to stay cool, but was nervous and fidgety. Roger got to work, because time was short and Clarke could be summoned away at a moment's notice. He was hesitant at first, but a few words from Roger put him at ease. He started to talk.

Clarke told Roger his side of the story, though I suspected that he didn't know that his new best friend was a journalist from Britain's top-selling newspaper. My chair was positioned nearby and I could hear most of their conversation. Alastair moved around the room, as he sneaked shots of Clarke and Roger. The room was busy with detectives checking records and clerks with forms to be filled in, but Roger had taken command. It was an impressive performance. He insisted that he must finish questioning the suspect before anyone else spoke to him, and the officials accepted his word.

Suddenly, the door swung open, and a television crew and reporters burst into the room. They launched a barrage of questions. Clarke looked terrified and covered his face with a newspaper. Roger went mad. He pushed me forward to face the mob from the media. "Deal with them," he said.

I was perplexed at my promotion but turned to face a scrum of charging reporters and television cameras with bright lights. Holding up my hands, I advanced, and the invading forces appeared to halt and stared at me for an instant. Mysteriously, they retreated, while some journalists offered half-hearted resistance.

"Who are you?" one television reporter yelled, while his lights man shoved the spotlight on me.

"Are you his lawyer?" someone else shouted out.

"No comment," I replied confidently. "You can't stay here. You must leave now."

Astonishingly, they complied. I was surprised at my new-found powers of persuasion

Inside the room, Alastair got to work in earnest. He positioned himself beside Roger, and moved closer without distracting him. Clarke produced an address list of customers, pages and pages of people in Britain who had written to Paradise Express for a catalogue of pleasures promised by "Adult Disneyland". Roger summoned one of the detectives and insisted that the document must be copied immediately, while the police officer, in turn, grabbed one of the clerks. The man rushed off on his assignment.

Bedlam erupted again as the reporters and television crew forced their way back in. They yelled out questions to Clarke at the other end of the room. He yelled back. The chaos was observed with bemused detachment by NBI detectives who wandered in and out of the room.

Clarke was now holding his own impromptu press conference, telling anyone who would listen that he was a victim of a religious cult, Jubilee Campaign, and an Irish priest, "a troublemaker", and that he'd been set up by "Danny Smith". Clarke swore on his daughter's life that he was innocent. It was evident that he had heard about ITV's news report but hadn't seen it or he would have recognized me.

The television crew cornered Shay in one part of the room and recorded an interview, while Roger told Clarke that he was a journalist. Clarke took it on the chin, unfazed, and distilled a "message for British readers". He repeated his "I'm innocent and I've been set-up by unscrupulous cult members" dispatch.

At one point, while in conversation with Roger, Clarke turned to me and extended his hand. "I didn't get your name," he said.

"Dan," I replied, enigmatically. It's my given name, rarely used.

Roger had finished his interview with Clarke and decided that it was time to move on. We left Shay with the media buzzing around him, and headed for Angeles City, about two hours away.

On the journey, Roger kept us enthralled with the backstory of scoops and exposés that he'd reported. Tabloid journalists have a bad reputation, but his perspective was that fame, greed, money, deceit, and revenge were the main motives that drove people to the media with secrets about former friends and chance encounters. Over the last decade, he had been a crusading journalist exposing the crooked and wayward among celebrities, churchmen, and politicians. His reports had resulted in arrests and deportations and, in one instance, in Colombia, almost ended in his assassination after his run-in with a drug baron. He had raced to the airport and caught the first plane leaving the terminal without knowing its destination.

Roger had exposed members of the Paedophile Information Exchange, a notorious network in the seventies who legally organized themselves into a group to campaign for public acceptance. With influential supporters across society, Roger gave us tantalizing clues to people still active.

Alastair had his own tales about the tabs and the ride passed quickly. We checked in at the Oasis, one of the better hotels in Angeles, but still a dump. It was common to see local girls returning with foreign guests. Downtown, the clubs were sleazy, the girls young, with foreigners everywhere. Roger went out on the prowl, hoping that the trail would lead to "The Target" he was pursuing, with a link to a television soap star. Getting the story into the paper depended on his success with The Target.

He returned at midday. The Target had agreed to meet that night. Roger and Alastair were part of the cover story that had been concocted. I was out of it. "Sorry, mate," Roger said. "Next time." The encounter was going to happen at the Cock and Bull, a sleazy go-go bar on the strip owned by a British expat. Roger told me that he would return at 9.30 p.m. to pick me up from the hotel to follow up some other leads. If I chose to go to the Cock and Bull, he would try to make contact and draw me into the circle. I considered the options but decided to stay at the hotel.

Roger returned at midnight, three hours late.

"You won't believe what happened," he said, charging into the room. Walking around in an agitated state, he related a convoluted but astonishing story.

Roger met The Target through the owner of the Cock and Bull bar whose confidence he had won by claiming to know Paradise Express's business partner (John Smith, in London). Every story that Roger told was linked to Paradise Express and John. The trick worked because the club owner also knew John. As a result of this fictitious connection, Roger was welcomed into the circle and The Target started to talk. A local photographer clicked away, light bulbs flashing. It worked like a dream. The set-up had taken several hours but it was in the bag.

Almost.

Roger set the scene for me. He and The Target were with the owner of the Cock and Bull in his club. Roger was buying. They raised their glasses, again. Party time.

A stranger walked into the bar and over to Roger, The Target, and the club owner. The club owner exclaimed, "John! What are you doing here?"

"I've just flown in. Who's this?" John asked, and pointed at Roger.

The Target slammed his glass on the bar, going crazy. "Whaddya mean? This is Roger, your friend from Thailand."

"Friend? I've never seen him before in my life!"

It was Michael Clarke's business partner from Paradise Express, John Smith, who had just arrived from London. Roger's cover story was about to explode.

The next few minutes were tense. The owner of the Cock and Bull called on local muscle. Roger and Alastair were surrounded.

With seconds to spare, Roger declared conspiratorially, "I'm going to tell you everything. I'm really after Michael Clarke. He owes me money and I'm going to get him."

Alastair was introduced as Roger's "hit man" who would earn his wages if Clarke didn't pay up.

Somehow they made it out of the club.

Roger explained that Alastair had been unable to get photographs of The Target, but they used a local photographer,

Ricky Lee, who hung around the clubs and bars, to shoot the incriminating pictures. They had to get prints. Without prints, the *News of the World* would not run the story. The hunt was on now to find Ricky Lee and to get the photographs that he had taken earlier that night. If The Target, John, or anyone else realized what was happening, no one would leave town.

Roger, Alastair, and I jumped in a cab and headed downtown. Our assumption was that the Paradise Express business partner had flown in from London to clean up the Filipino end of the operation.

Roger told me that John had brought a copy of ITV's news report on video with him. Like a light bulb exploding before us, we realized that if John had a copy of the news video, then he knew what I looked like since I was in the TV report. But I would be unable to recognize him. Roger pointed a finger at me and grinned. If I had gone down to the club and had been with Roger when John burst in, his cover story wouldn't have lasted seconds.

We had to move fast. Find Ricky Lee, the photographer. Get the film. Get out.

We hit the clubs. Things were still buzzing. But Ricky Lee wasn't in any of the bars. The only place we hadn't checked out was the Cock and Bull. Alastair agreed to step back into the danger zone. He packed a swagger, acted out the role of Roger's "hit man", and was back in minutes with the news that Roger's cover story was holding. Just. But, no photographer.

Finally, we met a bouncer from one of the clubs who recognized Roger and told him that Ricky Lee had gone home around midnight. The bouncer knew where the photographer lived and offered to pick up the roll of film and a deal was struck. Half the money now. The other half when the bouncer produced the film. They arranged to meet at the Oasis at noon.

It had been a late, late night, and no one spoke on the taxi ride back to the hotel.

Front-page news

I've never liked early mornings and when Alastair phoned my room at 8 a.m., I grumbled. Roger had showered and was in the lobby. Like a good newspaperman, he had all the dailies with him and Clarke's arrest was blasted across the front pages of most of them. The *Philippine Star*'s report stated:

> Travel agent Michael Clarke, 49, wept when confronted by NBI agents at Luz's Place in Baloy Beach.
>
> "I deny all allegations made against me," Clarke of Eastbourne in Sussex, said in a statement. "I swear to God and on my only daughter's life that I am telling the truth."
>
> An NBI agent said they still had no evidence against Clarke and could not charge him criminally. Sen Ernesto Herrera, however, urged the NBI to use video footage of Clarke taken by the Independent Television [News] which could implicate the Briton.
>
> Clarke claimed the video footage had been "doctored" by a certain Danny Smith who belongs to a religious group called Jubilee Campaign.
>
> Herrera had alerted the NBI about Clarke and contacted Columban priest Father Shay Cullen, who operates a child protection programme at the Preda Foundation. Preda members led the NBI agents to Baloy Beach.

All the papers carried the story. Clarke denied the charges. He had been set up. He had been set up by Danny Smith. He had been set up by a religious cult, Jubilee Campaign. He had been set up and the police had no evidence to charge him. He had been set up.

Clarke's case was the talk of the hotel in Angeles. I overheard two guys at the bar discussing what they would do to the villain who had framed him.

I didn't linger.

In court in Olongapo

Roger decided he would wait in Angeles City for the bouncer with the photographs from the Cock and Bull. He needed a final meeting with The Target. It was high risk but he had to get one last quote after revealing that he was a reporter.

Alastair and I hit the road to Olongapo City where Shay was expecting us. The rolling hills and greenery were pleasant and Alastair was talkative in the car. "What do you want? Fame? Fortune?" he asked me directly. "Are you a do-gooder or a religious fanatic?" He was a cynic, suspicious of people like me, and named the frauds and hypocrites he had encountered while working in the media.

I told him that my family and my faith were the important things in my life, but I understood his frustration with Christian groups who treated people like him as "projects".

Alastair said that his material possessions mattered most to him. "It's about how much money I can make," he told me. "Getting there before anyone else. Beating them to the punch."

We talked about people's motivation for doing things and considered that even the hardened outlaw was seeking redemption, although they didn't know it. We talked about Martin Scorsese's movie *Taxi Driver*, and the loner, Travis Bickle (Robert De Niro), who became obsessed with a child prostitute (Jodie Foster) and decided that his life's work was to rescue her from the clutches of her pimp.

"Perhaps a day will come," I told him, "that you will care about something, that you will want to help someone. And when that day comes, you'll remember this conversation."

"No," he laughed. "Not me. That day isn't in my calendar."

We decided on a pint of Guinness to settle the bet.

Olongapo had the eerie atmosphere of a lost, forgotten city that's been left to decay slowly. American fifties-style automobiles lay rusting by the side of the road, shiny Jeepneys picked up passengers who stood by rickety buildings with paint peeling off the walls, while familiar global advertising brands such as Coca-Cola promised that "Everything's gonna be all right."

We reached Shay's mission at midday. The Preda Foundation was set up by Shay and an outstanding couple, Lex and Merle Hermosa. Together they had developed a remarkable organization defending people's rights, establishing successful fair-trade products and an effective rehabilitation programme for exploited children. Even Alastair was impressed. Shay's one-room office/home had a veranda with a spectacular view of the bay, where we were served the best fried fish I'd ever tasted, with delicious fresh mangoes for dessert.

The phone rang. It was Roger in Angeles. The bouncer with the photographs didn't show. Alastair had to return to Angeles to try to get photos of the suspects. The paper couldn't run the story without photos.

Within the hour, Alastair had gone, and Shay and I caught up with the news. We were on the balcony when the phone rang, but he was back, minutes later, frowning. Another threat, but he shrugged it off. Ten minutes later, the phone rang again. The latest news was that Michael Clarke might be released. This galvanized him into action, writing letters to politicians, police authorities, newspapers. The fax machine pumped the protests into the night.

I left him at the fax machine.

* * *

The next morning everyone was up early as Preda staff busied themselves preparing for another day in court against two offenders: the Australian, Victor Fitzgerald, and a Frenchman named Charlie Luton.

Fitzgerald was the Australian tourist who had sailed into Subic Bay and dropped anchor unknowingly just below the Preda Foundation. Shay had been on the balcony when he spotted children on board a yacht with a *farrang* (foreigner). Filipino law prohibited young children from being in a private place with a foreigner who wasn't a blood relation. That was the law; it wasn't always enforced.

Shay grabbed a pair of binoculars and trained them on the yacht and this confirmed that there were young children on the vessel. Realizing something wasn't right, Shay phoned the police. However, they were reluctant to act. Shay wasn't surprised. Sometimes officials preferred to handle such encounters quietly, giving the offender the opportunity to buy his way out of a tight spot. With the Australian's yacht docked so close, Shay had been adamant. "Arrest him now or I will do it myself – a citizen's arrest."

Victor Fitzgerald was caught on board with three children, one about seven years old or younger. The entire incident was captured on video, including the exchange between Shay and the reluctant police officer.

Accusation and counter-accusation had complicated matters, but eventually Fitzgerald was charged with attempted rape against a young teen called Gloria. Her family were pressured to get her to drop the charges, and, to ensure that she could not attend a crucial court hearing, they manacled her feet with a dog chain and locked her in an outhouse. With the leading witness missing, the case would have been dropped and the suspect allowed to slip away. But after three days of captivity, Gloria escaped by climbing through a window and hobbled to the Preda Foundation, with the chains still around her feet.

Shay worked with the chief prosecutor and, despite intense pressure from the defence, Fitzgerald eventually faced the court. This hearing was critical as Shay's videotape of Fitzgerald's arrest was due to be screened for the judge.

The courtroom was a short journey from the foundation and Preda's investigators were on hand. It took two workers to carry the bulky television set into the courtroom while Shay guarded the videotape. The courtroom was a small room with a porch, six rows of benches, and a raised platform for the judge.

It was hot inside the courtroom, so we stood under the low roof outside, seeking shelter from the blazing heat. Fitzgerald and the Frenchman, Charlie Luton, arrived in a police vehicle, but both wandered around unchecked. Luton was surly but Fitzgerald looked harmless. He was friendly with the guards, strolled over to the tea shop across the road, bought a coke, meandered back and forth.

Fitzgerald sauntered over to me and started a conversation, while I played the part of a curious onlooker. Nothing he said was surprising, and predictably, he blamed everything on Shay, whom he cursed frequently, calling him a "correspondent from *Time* magazine". He let slip that he had a daughter studying in London, and mumbled, "But my family don't want to know me. That bastard has ruined my life." He cut a forlorn and dishevelled figure, and I felt a twinge of sympathy as a shadow of doubt crept in. Could this apparently kindly old man have been misunderstood?

Word came down the line that Fitzgerald's hearing had been postponed. The Preda workers were frustrated, convinced that it was a tactic employed by the defence attorneys to defragment the prosecution's case, in the hope that it would eventually be forgotten.

There was a flurry of activity as the judge summoned the courtroom to order. Fitzgerald sat in the front row beside Luton, whose case started despite several requests for postponement from his attorney. Gloria was the leading witness against Fitzgerald and sat on a bench alongside us, two rows behind the suspects.

Luton had an icy stare and looked tough. Preda staff told me that he was a karate expert, with a military background, and was rumoured to have served with the French Foreign Legion. He had apparently admitted to killings back home, and had been jailed in France for sex offences. Everyone called him "Crazy Charlie".

Crazy Charlie was annoyed with me because I had taken his photograph while he sat outside in the tea shop with Fitzgerald, and he had complained to a police officer. In court, he continually made eye contact with me, stared, walked across the room and taunted me with a piece of paper. He walked with a swagger and appeared to be the most confident person in the courtroom.

He had been charged with sexually abusing Allen, a young boy whom he had legally adopted in Olongapo. Allen, a tiny figure, aged about ten or eleven, walked forward to give evidence, and hunched over in the witness chair. Towering over him, Luton's attorney spoke in a loud voice, and repeatedly pointed his finger at the child. The chief prosecutor was impressive and the judge sympathetic; Luton's attorney was admonished for his grandstanding. He seemed to take little notice.

The ordeal was over and Allen stepped down from the witness stand but was forced to pass both Luton and Fitzgerald, seated in the front row. As he walked past, the child threw a piece of paper at Luton, in rage and frustration, and then crumpled in tears on a bench behind us. Luton's lawyer succeeded in gaining a postponement, and a court hearing was set for three weeks' time.

Our day in court was over. Preda staff loaded the television and video machine into the vehicle as the noonday sun beat down.

Crazy Charlie came down the steps of the courtroom and headed directly for me, his eyes cold and steady. It seemed that a violent confrontation was inevitable and I prepared for some kind of assault. He walked right up to me till we were almost touching, his eyes fierce with anger, never leaving mine, and yelled at me. He demanded to know who I was and why I was taking his photograph. He continued to stare, eyeball to eyeball. I couldn't tell who else was nearby but held my ground, and after a few minutes, he ended it by threatening to file a complaint against me. I challenged him to do so and he stormed off to find his lawyer.

Gloria came out of the courtroom. She was a slim, elegant girl, about thirteen or fourteen years old. Fitzgerald had been charged with attempted rape against her, and he watched her intently as she walked across our path and climbed into a maroon people-carrier vehicle. As the vehicle pulled out, I observed him closely. The body language and facial expression were unmistakable. He was enraptured, barely blinking, and watched the Space Wagon till it was out of sight. It was this eerie, menacing spectacle that convinced me his look of affection was not one of a parent but of a lover.

* * *

The next morning, a police vehicle with senior NBI officials from Manila pulled up unexpectedly at Preda's office. Shay and I sat down with the police officers on cane chairs in a room on the ground floor, with the fine linen curtains gently blowing in the breeze.

"What can you tell us about Michael Clarke and Paradise Express?" the NBI officer asked.

Shay's frustration was evident when it emerged that the case against Clarke was fading because of alleged police bungling. The tables were turned. The priest was quizzing the police. Had the police searched the house where Clarke was hiding? No. Did they know what had happened to the evidence that was in the house? It had probably vanished. Had they seen the promotional brochure from Paradise Express advertising an "Adult Disneyland"? No. How much did they know about Clarke? Very little. Had ITN's reporters given them the tapes of their interviews with Clarke? No. Did they know that Paradise Express's business partner, John Smith, had arrived in the Philippines and was currently in Angeles City? No.

I handed over copies of Paradise Express's advertisement from *Exchange and Mart* and the NBI officers examined it for the first time. Clarke had denied all the charges against him, insisting that he had been set up, but the officers agreed that the documents looked incriminating. We described the contents of ITV's news programme, and for the first time the police learned that Clarke had been recorded on tape, offering young girls for sex in the Philippines.

Shay urged them to move quickly and the NBI officers agreed to act on his advice. The NBI chief authorized me to try to collect the unedited video from ITV *News at Ten* and a letter, dated 10 June 1995, was prepared for me to carry back to London.

A big shock

On my last night in Olongapo, Shay drove downtown through the city's night life. Bars, massage parlours, and dance clubs were scattered around but the action was moving to Balloy Beach, now referred to as the "new Pattaya", Thailand's notorious sex district.

Shay pointed out a building where Clarke was arrested and then pulled up at a bar called Mr Pumpernickels. It was a scene straight out of an Elmore Leonard novel. The joint's owner, Harry Jost, welcomed us like old friends. Girls with heavily painted faces walked past. At the bar, a man with greasy long hair and tattoos on his arms eyed us without looking up. Two teenage girls, one in hot pants, the other a pink micro skirt, walked in, waved to Harry, and stood by the bar. Two ice cold San Miguels appeared mysteriously before them. The girls looked at us and giggled. Postcards from around the world were clipped to the side of the bar. Messages on cards and notes were pinned to a wooden post. A sign at the corner said, "Rooms to Rent". The jukebox blasted out a repetitive loop of songs, mostly disco.

Harry talked about arrests, kickbacks to corrupt politicians, wanted-men's secrets. He was called away to the bar and Shay whispered to me that he was the source who tipped him off about Clarke's hideout. When he returned, Harry said he knew where the girls featured in the TV news programme had been taken.

"I'm going to rescue the girls and bring them to Preda," he declared.

He had a lot of information about Clarke and spoke knowingly. Clarke had offered him a slice of the action and told him that they would make a lot of money from Paradise Express' clients. Everyone wanted to come on his tours. All Harry would have to do was to allow the sex tourists to stay at his place, hang out, have a beer, and of course, make sure young girls were available.

"Michael Clarke said he'd make a fortune, but the first customers he brought were reporters who exposed him," Harry laughed, and slapped his thigh.

Harry said he phoned the police and tipped them off about Clarke's hideout but they wouldn't arrest him. Chuckling, he turned to me and said, "Then I phoned Shay and he was here in twenty minutes."

On the way back, Shay explained that all was not as it seemed. He tried to unravel the plot, revealing that he'd been investigating Harry, who, in turn, had fallen out with his former cronies. Intrigue, ever present.

The following morning, Shay drove me to Manila and we spent a leisurely day in the city. The last few days had been busy but the trip was almost over and I settled in for an early night. I needed it.

The phone rang. It was Roger, back from Angeles City. He was excited; it had worked, and they got their photographs. It was going to be a big story, maybe even the front page. A splash.

"I'm bushed. We'll catch up at breakfast," Roger rasped down the line.

I said goodnight and turned out the light, the tiredness returning.

The phone rang. It was Alastair. "Can you come down to my room? You're not going to believe this."

Alastair seemed different somehow. Roger was in a chair looking wasted. A girl in a black-sequinned top and blue jeans sat cross-legged on the bed. Alastair stumbled through the story, his words tangled up in the rush to get them out.

"Frenzy's a dancer from a go-go bar in Angeles City. I want to save her. I want to buy her out of the club. I want her to go to college. I'm just not this kind of guy. It's crazy. She's not my girlfriend or anything. But I've been thinking about what you said and I really want to help this girl. Can Shay help?"

It was another late night.

Shay told me he would help if the girl was serious about getting out of the industry, but he'd seen it before. While most of the girls want to leave, many struggle with the demands of such a different life and, sadly, very few make it.

At breakfast, there was a confrontation between Roger and Alastair. Roger insisted that the first rule of journalism was not to get involved with "the story". "You've got to stay detached," he said.

He reviewed his own investigation of the last few days, speculating on the angles that the paper would be interested in. When he heard that I had told the police in Olongapo that John Smith, from Paradise Express, had arrived in the Philippines, he decided that Alastair should stay and photograph his arrest.

With a few hours to kill before our flight, I took a taxi to the mega mall for some last-minute shopping. Malls are a phenomenon in the Philippines and have taken the country by storm. There's a simple reason why they're so successful: air conditioning. This mall was the largest in Manila, six floors and as long as an airport runway. It was bewildering, all-encompassing, like a maze. Beyond the ritual of shopping, this had become an experience, and entire families spent the day there. I lasted eleven minutes and then ran for cover in one of the modest malls, but I just couldn't commit to buying anything.

Finally we boarded the plane. Roger was in the business section, I was in cattle class. He wanted to get me an upgrade but the flight was full. I tried to read but just couldn't concentrate.

As the silver jet soared into the sky, the roads and parks, homes and shacks, fields and hills started to shrink, resembling a grid on a computer game. I started to doze on the plane, fleeting thoughts coming through the ether on the fragility of life, the passing of time. It was another late night. This time I didn't mind. I was on my way home.

CHAPTER 4

You Can Run but You Can't Hide

The Media Sends a Strong Message, 1995–97

The *News of the World* hit the streets with a bang in the summer of 1995. Roger's investigation was splashed across the front page. Roger had done well. Although sensational in style, it was restrained in its detail. And there they were in the newspaper: Clarke, Smith, Fitzgerald.

With about 5 million people buying copies of the *News of the World* across the UK, Britain's top-selling newspaper guaranteed that people everywhere were talking about the child sex industry. The question people asked was: why doesn't the government do something about this scandal?

The television documentary about Shay's work that had been set up at the first meeting of the Street Children's Parliamentary Group (in 1992) was finally completed and screened nationwide in October 1995. Days before its broadcast, we previewed the hour-long programme for MPs and supporters in a packed room in Parliament.

A reporter in the film asked UK officials why they hadn't followed the FBI's example of investigating suspected offenders. The feeble response was, "The FBI asked for their addresses." The implication was that British officials hadn't even asked for addresses of suspects.

The reply caused spontaneous uproar at the meeting in Parliament. Nigel Griffiths MP turned to me and said, "If I was the Home Secretary, I would have been furious. I would have picked up the phone and expected a response on my desk the following morning."

I understood Nigel's outrage. He was the MP who had chaired our first meeting in Parliament three years earlier when we launched our campaign. Our report with Shay's list of suspects and offenders was published at the same meeting and we had passed this on to Scotland Yard. It was the same list that the TV reporter had followed up.

The front page

The media backed our campaign and Shay, Wilfred (our parliamentary officer), and I were regularly featured in a series of high profile news reports on television, radio, and in the newspapers. But there was still unfinished business, with 747 Travel operating freely.

Had Mike Stones and Peter Mitchell been following the media coverage? Were they trembling with fear of being exposed, or were they laughing because they had got away with it and were continuing to do so?

After a television interview, a reporter from the *Sunday Mirror* telephoned, "Can we work with you on your current investigation?"

It was time.

I handed the file marked "747 Travel" to the journalist and closed the door on ITN covering the story. The reporter offered money. "I don't want any money," I replied. "I just want this story told."

While some tabloid journalists seemed to enjoy a lurid reputation, in Jubilee Campaign's dealings "the tabs" were professional and ethical.

I followed the *Sunday Mirror*'s investigation from afar and on Sunday, 31 December 1995 awoke at 6 a.m. to buy the papers.

Staring back at me were pictures of Peter Mitchell and Mike Stones. The reporters had done their job: they asked the questions. And Mitchell and Stones went for it. Boastful, Mitchell was extensively quoted in the newspaper referring to child sex and encouraging the journalists to indulge themselves.

The *Sunday Mirror* had nailed them and I was pleased. If there was any doubt that the campaign to change the law was urgently needed, the newspaper had confirmed it with this investigation.

* * *

While the media maintained its public pressure, the government was also monitoring events unfolding behind the scenes in Ireland.

At his request, I flew over to join Father Shay in Dublin at a high-profile launch of the campaign to change the law there to prosecute sex tourists. Our lobbying materials and reports were widely used.

Owen Ryan, an active TD (Irish MP), heard one of the interviews and arranged an immediate meeting. Mr Ryan told us that he had drafted a bill as early as June 1995, but as a member of the Opposition Fianna Fail Party, he didn't want it to become a victim of political wrangling. "Child prostitution is a new form of slavery. It's outrageous that Irish citizens can be guilty of abusing children but escape punishment," he insisted.

In London, one of our supporters, Patricia Toomey, had been invited to the opening of the Irish Centre in Hammersmith to meet their special guest Dick Spring, Ireland's Deputy Prime Minister. Not wanting to waste an opportunity, Patricia placed Jubilee Campaign's report in Mr Spring's hand. "We need your help to change the law," she told him. Mr Spring assured her that he would read the report and seriously consider what she had said.

Five days later, Ireland's Minister of Justice, Nora Owen, telephoned Shay who had returned from the Philippines and was at his family home in Dublin. "We would welcome the bill even though it was from the opposition," she said.

At 7 p.m. on Tuesday 14 November, the bill was tabled in the Oireachtas (Irish Parliament) and Ireland joined America, Australia, Germany, Sweden, New Zealand, Belgium, France, Norway, and Denmark in endorsing legislation that was now sweeping the tourist-sending countries.

A TV journalist from Ireland's main channel, RTE, told me that the most extraordinary factor was that the government had accepted a private member's bill from the party in opposition – only the fourth in the history of the state. The contest for political supremacy was shelved and old adversaries united in the war against child prostitution and sex tourism.

The Irish bill was introduced amid strategic media coverage and effective lobbying. It was a moment for activists to savour, a personal triumph for Father Shay, and demonstrative proof that campaigning works.

It was Ireland 1, Britain 0.

The Daniel Handley murder

Brett Tyler was abandoned as a baby, raised in Barnardo's Homes, sexually assaulted at four, and in prison met his first "real" friend, Timothy Morss, who had also been abused as a child. Both had served time for sexual offences and became accomplices and lovers. In a special annexe of Wormwood Scrubs prison, the group therapy session for sex offenders heard the men discuss their ultimate fantasy, the final taboo – to abduct a young blond boy, abuse, and murder him.

When they left prison, Tyler flew to the Philippines to pursue his obsession with young boys. Meanwhile Morss became the lover of another former inmate, David Guttridge, and moved to Bradley Stoke, near Bristol, where they bought a house together. They also set up a minicab firm, Guy's Cars, in Camberwell, South London.

When Tyler returned to Britain (in April 1994), he teamed up with Morss and revived their secret fantasy. In October, the men went cruising. In East London, they spotted a young boy trying to fix the chain on his silver BMX bike.

"We were just looking at the boys, the usual hobby," Tyler would recollect later in his first police interview. "We saw a boy riding a bike. He took a side street so we turned round and went back. We pulled over, put a map in the back of the car, asked him to show us where we were and pushed him in."

The boy was Daniel Handley. He was blond. He was nine years old.

Daniel earned extra pocket money by collecting trolleys from the local Asda supermarket and helped people with their shopping. Daniel was allowed to ride his bicycle out on his own as long as he was home by 6 p.m. On Sunday 22 October 1994, he was late.

Tyler and Morss took Daniel back to Camberwell, and in the flat above the car hire firm they videotaped themselves abusing the child. Daniel was then driven along the M4 in Morss's Peugeot estate car, which pulled up in a lay-by close to junction 14. He was strangled with a knotted rope and buried in a shallow grave in woods adjoining Bradley Stoke, near the house that Morss shared with Guttridge. Two weeks later, Tyler and Morss returned to bury the body deeper in the ground. Both then took off for the Philippines. Tyler followed a similar pattern there, using a video camera to record his abuse, with a dozen videotapes as evidence. In one tape he is seen haggling over the price of sex and reducing it from the equivalent of 75p to 50p.

Tyler and Morss liked the Philippines because they could continue to abuse children and no one would know. They could get away with it. But eventually they fell out and Morss returned to the UK, where Daniel's disappearance had triggered a massive police hunt and intensive media coverage. Six months later, in March 1995, foxes disturbed Daniel's grave and a man walking his dog discovered his body.

In May, a BBC TV *Crimewatch* programme gave the hunt for the killers even more publicity, and the programme triggered memories from a psychiatrist and prison officer from Wormwood Scrubs. They rang the police the next day with the names of the wanted men.

But old-fashioned detective work had also paid off. As the police searched for links between East London and Bristol, they learned of the house in Bradley Stoke owned by Morss and Guttridge. Their names went straight to the top of the list of suspects.

Morss was arrested. The net was closing on Tyler and his days on the run were at an end. The police were given a clue: Olongapo City.

I was in the Philippines with Father Shay in 1995 when the call came through and followed events closely. It was from Superintendent Kevin MacTavish, a senior policeman attached to the Australian Embassy in Manila. He told Shay that Scotland Yard had sought his advice in helping to trace the wanted man. MacTavish could think of only one person who could track down the fugitive – Shay – and gave him the name of the man Scotland Yard were hunting:

Brett Tyler.

"I'll get straight on the case," Shay told the Australian lawman.

He put an experienced investigator on the trail and they located Tyler's hideout. At the time, some children were thought to be in the house. Tyler had won over the locals by paying for a few kids' school fees. He also posed as a priest and held church services in an outhouse. Shay asked for the full details of Tyler's house with possible escape routes and the information was passed down the line. Based on Shay's documentation, two Scotland Yard detectives flew out within days, and Tyler was arrested for immigration violations and deported for overstaying his visa. This was considered the only way to capture the suspected sex killer.

Tyler left behind incriminating photographs and letters. In one note, he wrote, "Kill the children for me."

One year later, as the case came to trial, prosecutor John Bevan told the jury, "You will hear evidence about as depressing an example of the dark side of human nature, man's inhumanity to man, and downright wickedness as you can imagine."

The tragic story of Daniel Handley caused a sensation. Like everyone else, Jubilee Campaign followed it. It provided the most dramatic example yet of how sex tourists could travel with impunity, and the ease with which they could conceal their movements. Even when arrested, Tyler had to be chased from the Philippines on an immigration offence. More importantly, he had abused children in Britain and the Philippines but he was hunted for the crime that he had committed in London. His crimes in Olongapo City went unpunished. This disturbing signal told men they could continue to travel abroad, abuse children, and get away with it.

* * *

The increasing media coverage, followed by the Irish bill, and now the Daniel Handley case, finally hit home. In 1996, the UK government did a sudden U-turn and announced that they would introduce extraterritorial laws for sex offences against children and would incorporate this into the 1997 Sex Offenders Act. Much of the legislation was modelled on the bill that Jubilee Campaign's parliamentary officer had drafted two years earlier.

The government also introduced a sex register for offenders. The Home Office intended to impose a three-month penalty for not registering, but our parliamentary officer recommended that this should be upgraded and consequently this was increased to six months' imprisonment and a stiffer fine.

When news broke about the change in the law, many of our supporters – and some journalists – called to share in our celebration at the success of this important campaign.

I was surprised that it had taken so long and had been such a struggle to convince the authorities. What could be more important than protecting our children?

High-profile cases, such as those of Sarah Payne and Milly Dowler, confirmed that abductions and sex crimes against children required further resources for the police and mechanisms for swift action. Crimes against children should be given equal priority as murder and terrorism.

Anyone who harms a child should get this message: you can run but you can't hide.

CHAPTER 5

Childhood Dreams

My Story, 1920s–1981

My grandfather, Captain Richard Elvidge, was an army officer during the British Raj who became infatuated by the vivacious personality of Effie Macmarquis, an accomplished pianist who performed and organized concerts for the troops in India. The soldier and the musician discovered they both had family in Dublin, and their romance turned to marriage. Captain Elvidge returned to England with his bride and managed the estate of his commanding officer, Lord Glanusk, in Crickhowell, Wales. When my grandmother became pregnant, Lord Glanusk insisted that her child should be the first baby to be born in a nursing home that he intended to set up for the local community. It was here that my mother, Eileen Alice, was born in February 1921; Lord Glanusk was named as her godfather.

When my mother was about seven years old Captain Elvidge lost all his money in a secret business deal and died of shock. Lord Glanusk offered to help the young widow and her child but my grandmother, with Eileen, decided that they would have a better life in India, where she had relatives who were doing well. So in 1928, my mother and grandmother set sail on the *City of London* bound for India.

When my mother's grandfather, John Macmarquis, in India, first set eyes on his young granddaughter, he was enthralled by her golden curls and beautiful green eyes. Mr MacMarquis had been personally awarded a medal by King George V in 1911 for his role as superintendent of the military cantonment in Indore and was an influential figure in the region.

Indore was a city from the old world that served as one of the engines that powered the wealth and dominion of the British Raj and accommodated several battalions of the British Army. The city encapsulated the fantasy of India, with ornate marble palaces and maharajas bedecked in embroidered robes; where Indian servants wearing gloves bore trays of iced lime juice for English ladies in summer frocks who sat under parasols on the veranda watching games of cricket or croquet being played on the lush green lawn. It was one of India's largest cities and John Macmarquis had control over the trade and industry of the area. But he never forgot the land of his birth; he listened to the wireless, and sympathized with Ireland's epic struggle for freedom from British rule. Young Eileen was captivated by the stories he related and was stirred by the first rumblings of conscience. This made quite an impact because, decades later, she would repeat them to me.

Meanwhile, my grandmother, Effie, set up her own school, taught music to the wives and children of the maharajas, and still found time to fit in the occasional concert. My mother was raised within the axis of the British Raj and taught to uphold and preserve English traditions, but her political consciousness was being awakened. In Ireland, rebels had launched an armed struggle for freedom. In India, the resistance harnessed an even greater force. This spirit of the struggle for justice was passing from grandfather to granddaughter and it stirred her youthful imagination. She learned to play the rebel Irish songs on the piano, and became a fervent student of Indian politics.

Mahatma Gandhi's campaign of civil disobedience made newspaper headlines worldwide. Gandhi was on a historic journey across India and when his freedom train stopped at their local station, Eileen, to her delight, was chosen to present the Indian leader with a garland of flowers. She told me it was an experience she cherished:

Even though it was a brief encounter, it was a moment that will always live in my memory. When the train pulled into the station, everyone crowded around. He travelled by third class to identify with the poor. Mahatma Gandhi had tremendous presence. I gained an inner confidence and walked forward and presented him with the bouquet of flowers. He smiled, thanked me, and put his hand on my head. I felt privileged and humbled at the same time.

When Jawaharlal Nehru was imprisoned by the colonial rulers, Eileen wrote to the activist, who was later to become India's first prime minister. She reminisced with me:

I told him that I had read all his books and supported the struggle for India's independence. I told him that I was just a teenager but that I was prepared to do anything to help. To my surprise, Nehru replied from prison, and over the next months we exchanged a few more letters. I followed the news closely and kept a scrapbook with cuttings about Gandhi and Nehru. India's fight for freedom and independence meant a lot to me.

After the death of her grandfather, my mother – now a young woman – moved to Calcutta, with her mother, and was energized by the big city. She joined a badminton club and developed an affection for a shy Anglo-Indian player called Walter Smith. Perhaps Walter was both the culmination and the embodiment of my mother's endless love affair with India, but with the blind passion of the headstrong and the innocent, they were married soon after in 1948. The arguments outlasted the marriage, and they separated before I was born the following year in Calcutta, the place Kipling called "the city of dreadful night".

I was named after the song "Danny Boy", but when my grandmother was filing my birth certificate, she wrote "Dan" because she considered it more of a proper name. I was always called Danny, and was frequently reminded that the popular song was considered an unofficial Irish anthem. Mum probably recalled the influence of her grandfather and perhaps this was a way of her youthful concerns living on after her. In fact, the song was composed by an Englishman, Frederic Weatherly, in about 1910, and adapted to the melody of "Londonderry Air" in 1913.

My earliest childhood memory was an incident in the street when my father tried to grab me and a scuffle broke out. Mum was assaulted as she tried to stop me from being taken. I learned later that the police were involved and a court case followed. I suspect Walter loved Mum but didn't know how to express it and was unable to resolve the conflict that had arisen between his wife and mother, who disapproved of the marriage.

I saw my father occasionally over the years but there were almost no moments of intimacy or affection between us. When one of his relatives came to tell me of his death when I was in my late teens, they expected me to be devastated but I only felt a dull sort of faraway pain. The sadness that came to me was not over his death but about the life that we had never known as father and son.

I didn't miss the absence of a parent growing up, as Mum made up for everything. She made my childhood garden a wondrous, magical place to grow. I lived a charmed life, with everything I wanted. I wasn't aware of the struggle and financial pressure she was under, as she worked to provide for us. It was years later that I discovered the extent of her sacrifice.

Mum worked several jobs to keep the family together. I was an only child but my grandmother lived with us, and for a while, her brother Charlie and two of his children, Betty and Pam, who were like sisters to me. Her main job at the time was with J. Lyons, where she worked as personal assistant to Sir Kenneth Gluckstein, one of the controllers of the tea empire. It was among the largest food manufacturing companies in the world and the Calcutta office was responsible for purchasing all the tea for export back to the famous J. Lyons tea rooms in Piccadilly, and elsewhere.

* * *

An article on the BBC website in January 2013 observed that Anglo-Indian culture was dying out, and asserted that celebrities Merle Oberon and Cliff Richard were among many Anglo-Indians who hid their origins. I understood how they felt because there were times when I felt that I didn't fit in. I didn't let this bother me too much since I felt drawn more to American culture.

I collected Roy Rogers comics, proudly wore my Davy Crockett coonskin hat, scared rustlers with my Colt Buntline special, a particular kind of revolver popularized by Wyatt Earp, the sheriff of Dodge City – and my teddy was named Randy after hard-riding, fast-shooting Randolph Scott. I breezed through Peanuts cartoons, *Mad Magazine*'s Don Martin cartoon strip, and was stirred by James Dean's moody characterization of Cal Trask in *East of Eden*. I memorized every move, and turned myself into a brooding, troubled teenager, even though I hadn't reached thirteen.

After hearing Elvis, I combed my hair back, and spent hours in front of the mirror trying to move like I'd seen him move in his early movies. RCA Victor didn't have a licensing deal in India so records by Elvis were rare and only available for a price. Elvis reminds me of my childhood, and, later in life, I returned to his music and understood the role he played in the evolution of popular music.

My first assignment

The biggest event in my life, aged about fifteen, was a concert by the jazz musician Duke Ellington in the early sixties. The concert was mesmerizing and I can still remember being transfixed by the throb of the full orchestra and the moment Ellington strolled on stage.

It was particularly thrilling because of the drama enacted behind the scenes. I had started collecting autographs as a young teenager, and I had bought a new autograph book to mark the occasion. I'd assumed that The Duke would be staying at the best hotel in town (the Grand) and this was confirmed by the front desk when they refused to put me through to his room. I was unprepared for the staff's distinct lack of enthusiasm for my enterprise. I was certain that the hotel's famous guest wouldn't be disturbed. The hotel disagreed. I was thrown out. But I sneaked back and my tenacity paid off as I wangled my way to the band's lead trumpeter, "Cat" Anderson. He talked to me as if I were a buddy and I left him, walking on cloud nine. I also left with the room numbers of the band. It took a few hours but eventually I had autographs from Johnny Hodges, Billy Strayhorn (the composer of Ellington's signature tune "Take the 'A' Train") and the biggest prize, Duke Ellington himself.

I suspect my friends were stunned that I'd pulled it off but it hadn't surprised me. I just hadn't considered the possibility of leaving the hotel without his autograph.

A few years later, the gospel singer Mahalia Jackson played a concert in Calcutta and I pursued her armed with the same autograph book. This time, I had an agreement that Calcutta's leading English-language newspaper, the *Statesman*, would publish my interview with her. It was my first assignment.

I loved the thrill and drama of both these encounters and the allure of meeting these musicians never left me but I hadn't thought this could become a job. It was too much fun.

Involvement with Operation Mobilization

School was boring. I studied *Melody Maker*'s pop charts more than any textbook, and manoeuvred an exemption from any Indian language classes; at the time, this seemed like an accomplishment.

I took some interest when word spread that a former student had hit it big as the "English Elvis", and years later, I reminded Cliff Richard of our shared history at La Martinere. I did the fashionable thing of dropping out to study art. After my pastel sketches were included in an exhibition at the Academy of Fine Arts, the *Statesman* named me as someone with potential, and I thought that art would influence the direction of my life.

My mother took me to church as a child and afterwards as a reward for not fidgeting too much, we'd go to the toy shop to pick up another Dinky toy from Meccano for my growing collection. I grew up with a general awareness of God and was taught to respect people of different faiths and those with none. I developed a personal faith after an unexpected encounter with George Verwer, the leader of Operation Mobilization (OM), a student Christian movement. Some people have called this a "born again" experience, though I came to regard it as a journey of faith and discovery rather than a state of arrival. I didn't think of myself as religious but my personal belief in God became an inheritance I carried through life.

I joined OM and travelled across India and Nepal with them during the mid/late sixties. It was this involvement that unveiled a side of the country that I had obscured from view, one that was different from the world of air-conditioned cinemas and night clubs that I was familiar with.

For some, India holds a mystical fascination, while others are dismayed by the ubiquitous poverty. When I was growing up, I was encouraged not to ignore the beggars and occasionally my mother would send support for Mother Teresa, the Catholic nun who cared for the poor and dying, but to me the devastation of Calcutta's destitute was overwhelming. Strangely, I found it easy to put it out of my mind. And when it did infiltrate the borders of my world, it felt as though I was in another country.

I heard George Verwer say, "We can't feed everyone in India but we must stop for the needy people we meet to show that we care." One day I was with him in Mumbai when a beggar stopped us. George talked to him and then together we walked in search of a shop selling food, but were stopped at the entrance. The manager stood in the doorway, "You, *sahibs*, can come in, but not that thing," he said, pointing to the beggar.

My first job at an international aid organization

Mum regularly made plans to return to the UK but the trip kept getting put off. It was always "next year in Crickhowell", and we finally made it in 1970 after I'd turned twenty. Not much surprised me in Britain, though I expected Carnaby Street to be bigger. I found work with George Bell, publishers of general subjects including *The Diary of Samuel Pepys*.

To launch their latest chess books, I organized a living chess match between Grand Masters Raymond Keene and Tony Miles and the event was promoted as a friendly competition between the political magazines *The Spectator* and the *New Statesman*. We borrowed costumes from the Mermaid Theatre's props and the colourful contest was staged at Lincoln's Inn Fields with various personalities taking part. The columnist Jeffrey Bernard commanded attention as a white knight wearing the horse headdress borrowed from Peter Shaffer's stage play *Equus*. Television and radio gave us good coverage and all the national newspapers ran photographs. I got a raise, but World Vision made me a better offer and I joined them in the late seventies to help set up their communications office in Europe.

World Vision had a historical interest in Cambodia. When the Khmer Rouge seized Phnom Penh in 1975, the dictator Pol Pot's brutal reign resulted in the death of 25 per cent of the population from starvation, overwork, and executions. After the Khmer Rouge were forced out, World Vision re-entered the country in 1979, and we were provided with the latest raw footage from inside the country. It was tough viewing but made my job easier as the television channels took the footage and we made headlines. I felt energized being part of such a worldwide story. It also gave me an insider's view into just how the game was played, by a multi-million dollar corporation, the "charity business" in the UK, and the treacherous media world.

The other big story of the day was the news that thousands of people were fleeing Vietnam in boats. Some were escaping political persecution; others just wanted a better life. There was a resistance to calling them refugees and a new phrase was coined: economic migrants. It started to get usage by the press and politicians and you could usually tell people's opinion by which word they used to describe the Vietnamese Boat People.

By July 1979, there were over 60,000 of them in camps in Hong Kong, still a British colony, and they were arriving at the rate of 500 a month. We were getting grim stories about the overcrowding in the camps and about the perilous journey in the South China Sea, as families fled in makeshift boats and small fishing vessels. Later, I had the opportunity to get into these camps and heard their disturbing stories first-hand.

The truth is, after reading the reports and hearing people retell what they had seen and heard, the personal tragedies lost their edge, and I became desensitized to the stories. They stopped being people, and became statistics. It was all about which story we could put out in a press release, and if there wasn't a suitable photograph, the story was spiked. If it wouldn't get used it wasn't worth spending time on. I looked for a photogenic child and knew this would catch someone's attention. The print media's coverage was strong but there hadn't been any in-depth television reports. I felt sure that the life-and-death struggles of these desperate families would make great television. Somewhere inside me, I also hoped it would do some good. I scribbled down a pitch and made some appointments. I went into negotiations with the BBC. It wasn't a hard sell, and the result (*Desperate Journey*) was one of the first hour-long documentaries that investigated Vietnam's Boat People and launched the BBC's *Everyman* series.

* * *

Was it chance, design, or as Bob Dylan put it, just a simple twist of fate? I never imagined that my mission in life would be to campaign for children at risk and victims of injustice.

Human rights had been a passing interest. I'd stood in the rain at a vigil outside the Soviet Embassy for imprisoned writer Vladimir Bukovsky, and attended protests by the Women's Campaign for Soviet Jewry. I'd also joined the former *New York Times* music critic Robert Shelton and another writer, Liz Thompson, to launch Joan Baez's human rights group, Humanitas, in Britain.

But in 1981, I had plans. Other plans.

My day job fitted in with chasing freelance interviews. The *Daily Mail* was enthusiastic about an interview I had done with Arlo Guthrie but they wanted a rewrite to emphasize the risk he faced of contracting Huntington's disease. His father, Woody (America's celebrated troubadour and composer of "This land is your Land"), had died from this hereditary disease, and Arlo had a 50-50 chance of getting it. I felt it should be part of the story, but not dominate it. We couldn't agree and I settled instead for *Melody Maker*, who published the article in May 1981 just as I had written it. I learned that Fleet Street wanted "hooks" for stories and that I didn't have the bones to be a tabloid journalist.

I lived in Abbey Wood, South London, but loved America and had spent as much time there as I could afford to in the mid-to-late seventies, after Noel Stookey (the "Paul" of Peter, Paul and Mary) invited me to his home "just across the road from the Atlantic Ocean" in South Blue Hill, Maine, to discuss a book about his life. Noel told me that the best things in his life had happened naturally. It was advice that I packed for the journey.

In New York City, one of Columbia's publicists ran through upcoming gigs by their rising artists and asked who I wanted to listen to. I chose Asleep at the Wheel. Their name had more zing than Bruce Springsteen.

At *Rolling Stone* magazine's Fifth Avenue office in New York, their publishing editor was enthusiastic about developing a book about my friend, Mike Porco, the owner of the legendary "Gerde's Folk City" in Greenwich Village. *New York* magazine said he'd "probably given more musicians a chance to make their stage debut than any other man alive". Mike became legal guardian to Bob Dylan, paid for his initial publicity photograph, and was the first to give him a paid gig. Robert Shelton's review in *The New York Times* helped land a recording contract for the aspiring singer-songwriter.

I'd turned thirty, and after leaving World Vision, I paid the mortgage by freelance work in publishing and the media but had my mind set on a career in music journalism. By this time, I'd encountered and interviewed people such as Little Richard, Ricky Nelson, Billy Preston, Roger McGuinn, Bruce Cockburn, Peter, Paul and Mary, John Denver, Gordon Lightfoot, Joan Baez (a few times), and in Los Angeles, finally, the elusive Bob Dylan.

Although authors of books about Dylan could probably fill a conference hall, I had mined a few nuggets of my own. Dylan first performed "Blowing in the Wind" at Mike's club but veteran producer Milt Okun told me that Harry Belafonte, the Chad Mitchell Trio, and others had rejected the song because it was "too political".

When another American publisher waved a contract in front of me for a book about Bob Dylan it was like a neon sign lighting up the road ahead. Early in 1981 I was developing outlines and transcribing tapes for books about him and Mike Porco when the telephone rang. It was Peter Meadows. He organized a large church event called Spring Harvest and published a youth magazine called *Buzz*.

"Are you interested in working on a new project we're launching at Spring Harvest?" Peter asked. He outlined a complex human rights story in Moscow of "the Siberian Seven".

My conditions were simple. "Three and a half days a week, with the option of working from home, strictly for two months," I replied. "And £500 a month."

I didn't think Peter would go for it, but after a pause, he said, "Can you start on Monday?"

It seemed relatively easy money and I didn't think an occasional visit to the magazine's South London office would prove too much of a distraction. I had no idea.

CHAPTER 6

Siberian Protest

Meeting the Siberian Seven, 1981

I took the job because I'd assumed it was easy money. Yet, there was something intriguing about the story. As I probed deeper into the Siberian Seven case, it seemed obvious that someone wanted it buried and forgotten.

I had followed the samizdat movement in Russia and had read Alexander Solzhenitsyn's chronicle of the labour camps system, *The Gulag Archipelago*. Western coverage of the protest of Russian writers and poets was considered helpful as publicity offered protection. Little did I know that the leader of the Siberian Seven had played a critical role in developing this strategy.

After the Bolshevik revolution in 1917, the authorities had cracked down on religion, as churches were closed and thousands of clergy and believers were murdered. President Nikita Khrushchev continued the assault in the fifties and promised to wipe out Christianity. The last Christian, he thundered, would become a relic to be ridiculed on public television.

Nowhere was this rage greater than in Chernogorsk, a small, coal mining town in Siberia. The Christians in this community, led by Peter Vashchenko, took a dramatic decision to organize the first demonstration ever held inside the country. Secretly, thirty-two Siberians travelled 2,000 miles to Moscow and burst into the American Embassy on 3 January 1963 to appeal for help from the rest of the world. Their demonstration created a sensation as the story hit the front pages in the West. It was the first indication that Christianity had survived communism's brutal offensive.

British author John Pollock was commissioned to investigate and his book, *The Christians from Siberia*, was the first to deal with the survival of the Christian faith after half a century of militant atheistic rule. He never met anyone from Chernogorsk but learned the name of the man who had organized the demonstration: Vashchenko.

Fifteen years later, in 1978, a couple working at the American Embassy in Moscow were reading Pollock's book and recognized the Vashchenko name. They were in for a surprise.

Peter Vashchenko, and seven others, returned to the American Embassy, in 1978, to seek advice about emigrating. When a Soviet guard at the gate stopped Peter's sixteen-year-old son John and wrestled him to the ground, the others dashed inside. Initially, they wanted help in rescuing John, but the American officials were reluctant to get involved. The Siberian families expected the Americans to be sympathetic to their reports of persecution. Instead, the US exercised a "get tough" policy and pressured the group to leave the building.

The Siberians feared reprisals from the Soviet authorities because each of them had experienced persecution. Peter Vashchenko and his wife Augustina had both been imprisoned for their beliefs, once at the same time, despite having young children at home. Their daughters, Lida and Lyuba, had been forcibly removed for "re-education" as teenagers.

Convinced they'd "disappear" if they left the embassy, the Siberians endured the hostility of their reluctant hosts. The Americans feared their embassy would be deluged if seen to help this group and moved the Siberians to a tiny, claustrophobic basement room, about 20 feet by 15. Sympathetic staff took them food. The deadlock intensified with each passing day and they were frequently threatened with eviction.

The couple in Moscow who were reading Pollock's book were astonished to learn that the Vashchenkos, named by the British author fifteen years ago, were back, and now lived like outcasts in the basement. They arranged for Pollock to meet them and a book was rushed out in 1979 hoping that the publicity might help their case. Pollock called his book *The Siberian Seven*.

Basement encounter, 1981

Three years later, Dan Wooding, a journalist from the *Sunday Mirror* (and author of some forty books) persuaded Peter Meadows to take up the case, and the "Campaign to Free the Siberian Seven" was launched at Spring Harvest in April 1981. Peter's ambitious idea was to hold a rally in Trafalgar Square to publicize the campaign. Ten days before the event, I suggested that Peter should go to Moscow. The scoop: the first interview with "the Seven".

Peter's eyes sparkled. "I'm busy," he said emphatically, but with a lazy grin, added, "What are you doing this weekend?"

When I called our travel agent, she laughed out loud. "You can't fly to Moscow and get back in time for your meeting at Trafalgar Square. We need ten to fifteen working days for a visa."

She explained the "Catch-22" situation regarding travel to the Soviet Union. You couldn't book a ticket without a visa, and you could only apply for a visa if you had a ticket. It seemed a conspiracy between airline and consul to make travel to the USSR as difficult as possible. Our demonstration in Trafalgar Square was scheduled for 27 June 1981. There just weren't enough days to get a visa, fly to Moscow, and return in time.

That evening, I complained to David Willis, who had been a foreign correspondent in Moscow when the saga of the Siberian Seven started. David drawled, "There's only one person who can get you a visa. His name's Barry Martin. He could be anywhere in the world. You'll probably never reach him but here's his telephone number."

I hung up and dialled the number. It rang three times and a husky voice answered, "Barry Martin."

I didn't know who he was (years later John le Carre would give him a nod in his novel *The Russia House*) but told him everything. "Will you help me?"

Barry asked a few questions and then paused. The waiting was excruciating.

"Be at my office near Oxford Street at seven-thirty tomorrow morning. Bring your passport and four photographs with you."

Within a few days, I had my visa and a ticket to Moscow.

Barry Martin had emerged like an angel from nowhere, making the impossible possible. There was no time to prepare; there were just things to do. Nothing was more important than arranging for my black cat, Durango Rolling Thunder, to be fed while I was on assignment in Moscow.

* * *

The Americans had forbidden anyone to meet the Siberian Seven but before leaving London, I'd been told of a sympathetic embassy official who might help. I flew to Moscow, willing to take that chance.

"Come on down," my contact said on the telephone.

Moscow taxi drivers broke all the rules and created some new ones. Rusty Skodas raced through red lights, sending innocent pedestrians scurrying to the pavement. Capitalistic concepts were alive and well in the communist capital. A taxi journey from my hotel to the American Embassy on Chaikovskova Street varied from one to ten roubles, depending on the route. Frequently, I got the grand tour.

Twenty minutes after my phone call, I waved my passport at the Russian guards, and walked through the American Embassy gates, as though this was part of my normal routine. Inside the courtyard, I followed the instructions and found the lift. The lift had just one button. It stopped on just one floor – his floor. My contact was a senior military official, probably a CIA spook.

George Powell greeted me with a firm handshake. "Let's go for a walk," he said, and we headed back to the lift. George was sympathetic: "I'd like to help but I doubt if you'd get permission to see them. No one else has."

We walked on in silence, and then George said mysteriously, "There may be another way."

George sketched the layout of the building on my notepad and pinpointed the basement room. "The rest is up to you," he grinned. "Of course, I've never seen this paper before."

As we walked, George pointed out men who he claimed were KGB agents. Someone in a black leather jacket approached us, and said to me, "English." It was a statement, rather than a question. Not waiting for confirmation, his face grimaced, he gripped his chest as if he'd been shot, and in a tortured voice, exclaimed, "John Lennon!" Without another word, he straightened up, and walked on as though nothing had happened.

The embassy building was bugged so George regularly debriefed "couriers" during such walks and expected our stroll in the sun to have been monitored. "The KGB may assume that you've brought me a hot tip," he cautioned. "Be careful. We're in a cold war."

I followed George's directions and located the dark winding corridor, past the barber shop, and finally saw the basement room, with its open door. The Siberians were unprepared for my sudden arrival but within a short time, I was welcomed within their circle as a friend.

Peter Vashchenko's daughter, Lyuba, aged twenty-eight, had taught herself English, while Lida, their eldest daughter, I was to discover, was perceptive and subtle. Lilya, the youngest at twenty-four, was simply charming. In another context, she would have young men leaving flowers at her door.

"See, not everyone dislikes us," Lilya said, pointing to a stray cat which had taken up residence in the basement with them.

The Vashchenkos shared the space with Maria Chmykhalov and her young son, Timothy. At times, things were tense between the families. Maria divided her time between knitting, writing letters home, and reading the Scriptures.

Over the next few days, my priority was to call on foreign correspondents to advocate that, after three years, these "hostages of conscience" deserved coverage. Andrew Nagorski from *Newsweek*, had recently arrived in Moscow and was unaware of the drama. The *Daily Telegraph*'s Nigel Wade was enthusiastic. "Third Anniversary? No, I didn't know. Yes, come on down." Michael Binyon from *The Times* invited me to his high-rise apartment and talked about the phenomenon of reporting from inside a censorship machine. "It's like living on another planet," he enthused. He told me a quirky anecdote (included later in his book *Life in Russia*): a newspaper in Birlyusy in Siberia hadn't appeared for a whole month. No one complained, no one noticed. When I asked Binyon if he wanted to leave Russia, his reply was instant, "Gosh, no, there's nowhere else I'd rather be."

Barry Martin had booked me into the National Hotel, an ornate, rambling building just off Red Square. That evening, a string of anonymous phone calls left me puzzled. They seemed to be coming from the room next door, where earlier I'd noticed a tough young man in a black leather jacket loitering in the doorway.

I opened a window. The fresh air felt good. I decided to explore the city. The buildings were drab, cold, grey blocks of stone, assembled at random. The people seemed preoccupied, morose, their eyes distant; they caught your gaze and then looked away. I strolled on, oblivious to everything around me, walking without purpose, following my feet.

Within five minutes, two men had accosted me in separate incidents. Both were dressed in a kind of standard issue black leather jacket, and they appeared to have information about me. I dismissed these chance encounters and brushed aside the second man like a pet dog.

Back at the National I was faced with the bad news that I'd missed dinner. It took skill, ingenuity – and some foreign currency

– to secure the promise of food. When dinner was served, I was dismayed. The fried egg was stuck to the plate and had to be scraped off. Several minutes later, the butter arrived. It looked as if the leftovers from everyone else's plate had been dumped on mine.

Still hungry, I left the dining room in search of food and stumbled into the bar. "Dollars! Dollars!" came the command when I tried to buy chocolates with a five-pound note. A friendly barman came to the rescue and a deal was struck.

The bar was a large, dimly lit room with high ceilings and a gloomy atmosphere. Within minutes, two young Russian girls appeared at my table. They seemed curiously well informed about my trip, while their questions seemed rehearsed. Juliet pressed herself against me and whispered details about the pleasures I could expect if I would accompany them to "some other place close by".

A British film crew were nearby, and Andy, the sound technician, told me that Moscow was "unbelievable". I nodded knowingly. At another table, a group of businessmen fawned over a strikingly attractive girl with a voluptuous figure wearing a scarlet dress the size of a handkerchief. I'd assumed she was a starlet shooting a movie in Moscow.

The man from the room next to mine sauntered into the bar, collected a bottle, and left. His presence seemed to create a nervous tension among the staff.

I was at the bar when I felt a hand on my wrist. It was the film star in the scarlet handkerchief. "I know you," she pouted, speaking with a harsh accent. "You born in India but you travel with Irish passport. Why you do that?"

She spoke her words like a fortune teller at a country fairground. There wasn't any build-up, no sense of mystery, no tantalizing clue, but her words dazzled me with the kind of shock and suspense on which Alfred Hitchcock had built his legendary career. Although the other strangers I had encountered hinted with casual, ironic remarks, this was undoubtedly someone who had access to information about me.

I extricated myself from the girl with the movie star looks and returned to my table where Juliet was waiting. She launched a final offensive to entice me out of the hotel, but accepted defeat with a compromise. "At least, telephone me," she said sullenly, and scribbled her number in my notebook.

That night I was awoken around 3 a.m. by the telephone. No one spoke. The hotel was quiet but I could hear someone moving around next door. I checked that my door was bolted and pulled on my clothes and shoes. Somehow it gave me confidence, though, strangely, I didn't feel afraid.

Sometime the next afternoon, I made it to John Osman's apartment. The BBC's veteran reporter was brilliant and agreed to cover the story. Before leaving, I told him about recent encounters: the US intelligence agent; men in black leather coats; the suspected honeytrap at the hotel. He asked a few pertinent questions, and then said, "I think they're going to pick you up."

"What? Arrest me?" I was flabbergasted. This had never occurred to me.

"Probably," John replied. "If so, I'll broadcast the arrest on the radio, reveal why you've come to Moscow, and explain that you're not a spy."

It had become another story, and he knew exactly what to do. He made a note of my passport details. John thought that the surveillance, obvious in the extreme, was meant to intimidate me. "They want you to know that they're watching you."

"I don't know what to do next," I mumbled.

"Just carry on as usual," John advised. "I'll get you out of prison."

John arranged for me to telephone him regularly. "This is serious," he said. "You must call me wherever you are. If you haven't called, I'll assume you've been arrested. I want to broadcast the news within an hour of your arrest. It's important."

Outside, everything seemed calm. Across the street, two men sat in a black car parked at the curb. Were they plain clothes waiting to grab me and bundle me into the boot? Would they pull me off the street in broad daylight? Why were this couple staring at me from the corner? Was the empty taxi that cruised past a decoy? It was like a movie.

I hailed a taxi and directed him to Chaikovskova Street. At least I would be safe at the embassy. This was my final chance to see the Siberian Seven on my last night in Moscow.

On the run

Peter Vashchenko sounded alarmed. He was convinced that my links with the embassy had made me a target. He told me that the Russians wanted revenge for a recent shooting between British and Russian agents. "It's dangerous for you," he warned. "They could make you disappear – just like that!" He snapped his fingers as Lyuba interpreted his words.

In the tiny basement room, with daylight slowly fading, their hushed voices chronicled accounts of spies and surveillance; some were dramatic, many were personal. They told me that there were over twenty listening devices in their room, and that many of the Russian staff at the embassy spied on the Americans.

The Siberians had recently been allowed outside for an hour each day, and Maria Chmykhalov pulled a mauve patterned shawl around her shoulders and headed for the door, as the others followed.

Alone in the room, I thought a photo of the Siberians outside the room was a brilliant idea and I set off to find them. I walked down the corridor leading to the back of the embassy building and saw them at the end of the courtyard.

Lyuba spotted me first. I could tell she was annoyed. Her eyes made signals my mind couldn't read. I handed my Pentax ME Super to Timothy and outlined some poses. I was enjoying playing art director, and wondered how Annie Leibovitz would shoot them.

"Can I help you? Sir!" someone called out.

"No, it's fine," I replied jauntily. I was having fun and didn't need anyone meddling, particularly some amateur.

The marine asked who I was visiting. I replied nonchalantly, "I'm visiting the Vashchenko and Chmykhalov families."

He grimaced. "The Siberians!" He virtually spat out the words. "Have you been in the basement?"

Still, oblivious to any danger, I sailed in, "Yes, I've visited them."

"Do you realize that's a restricted area?" His tone turned aggressive.

"No," I said, casually. I was in the American Embassy and he was a marine. He wasn't the KGB.

He stared intently at me. "You must leave immediately. You are not to have any further contact with the Siberians. You must not return here. Do you understand me? Sir!"

It felt as though I had been struck.

"Do you understand me?" his voice lowered in tone as he inched closer towards me.

"Yes," I answered, clearly shocked. "But I've got to say goodbye to my friends."

"Permission refused," he said, the marine and I almost touching. "You must leave now."

"But my passport, coat, money... everything I have is in their room," I protested.

The marine and I had reached an impasse. Finally he broke the silence: "Collect your things and leave immediately." He was emphatic. "Don't return."

I expected someone to step from the shadows and go "Joke!" But no one did.

My throat was dry and I felt slightly dizzy. Each step seemed to require great effort. It felt as though I was walking underwater. There was an irony here, I knew it, but it was hard to focus. Someone was writing a message in the sand, but before I could read it, the tide flowed in and washed the words away.

The KGB had mistaken me for a spy because of my links with the American Embassy, and I was on the wanted list of the Russian secret police. But the Americans were treating me like a criminal, evicting me from the one place that I thought I'd be safe, forcing me onto the streets and into the clutches of the KGB. How had things got so tangled? There was just no one to turn to. I was alone, a target for both the KGB and American security.

It was dusk and a low smoky light bathed the courtyard in a dull glow. I whispered a prayer and walked quietly back to see the Siberians who had left the courtyard. They looked forlorn as I explained what had happened.

"But where will you go? It's not safe for you in Moscow," Lyuba said, articulating the obvious. Night was almost on us, and I didn't want to return to the streets of Moscow or to my room at the National.

Peter Vashchenko took charge. "It's dangerous for you on your own. You will stay with us tonight." It was an electrifying moment.

"My greatest fear is that the Americans will take revenge and punish you," I said, speaking as softly as I could, to the others who had huddled round.

"My greatest fear is that the Russians will take revenge and punish you," Peter said, brushing aside my protests.

It had been an extraordinary day. Just when I assumed that there was no shelter, help had come, beyond anything that I could have expected, at a risk none of us could afford. People with nothing had offered everything they had.

When would the marine check that I had left the room? How would this tiny cramped room accommodate me when it was too small for them? And what punishment would the Americans foist on the Seven if they discovered what they intended to do? The door to their room was always open. Anyone could walk in at any time. The marine on guard duty checked on them without warning.

Timothy and Lilya kept lookout, watching from the corridor. If anyone approached, I was to go into the bathroom with one of the girls who would pretend to take a shower. Would it work? Who could tell?

"Come, eat," Augustina, Peter's wife, smiled, handing me a plate of delicious fried chicken. Few words were spoken as the evening chores were completed. There were a few close calls, and Augustina suggested that we get to bed early to minimize the risk.

Chairs and boxes were moved, sleeping bags unrolled as Peter and Timothy worked quickly. Peter spoke with authority, "This is where you will sleep. No one will find you here."

It didn't seem possible, but, incredibly, they performed an act of creative genius in their small room. Where seven people slept, space was found, and an actual hiding place was crafted. The table against the wall was pulled forward slightly to allow space between it and the wall. Then cardboard boxes, clothes, and books were piled up around the legs of the table. In the hollow, a crawl space had been created. Timothy tried it out. It was true: you couldn't tell that a body was hidden behind it.

And for a single night, I joined them and we became "the Siberian Eight". This incident would remain our secret, never revealed till now.

But there was one final act before bedtime. With the door wide open, we knelt on the cold floor, in the centre of the room, as Scriptures were read, voices raised in prayer. I've never known a moment of such vulnerability or such power.

I crawled into position behind the table, and Peter and Timothy moved the boxes over me.

"It's perfect," Peter smiled, as he knelt on the floor beside me. "God has given us the power to keep you safe."

The room had offered up a hiding place and I sheltered in its secret.

Maria slept on one bed, Peter and Augustina on the other. Space was cleared in the middle of the room, as all three girls spread makeshift mattresses on the floor. Timothy slept in the corridor. He woke me the following morning, and we quickly returned the room to its normal state.

We said goodbye in the dimly lit hall just outside the basement room. Each one clasped my hands, whispering words of encouragement. My words seemed frozen. "I'll never forget you," was all that I could mumble.

At the National, I threw my clothes into the suitcase, checked out of the hotel, and headed for the airport. I didn't want to spend an extra minute in Moscow.

But there was to be one final twist. All the film in my hand luggage was ruined. The only film that could be developed was from a roll that I carried in my waistcoat. At the deserted airport lounge, I had been distracted for a few minutes and barely noticed two young men moving furtively. It was mystifying.

All the way back I was haunted by that basement encounter. Not a depression, but a sadness. I was on a flight to London, changing planes in Paris. Back to family, friends, home. With the tables turned, my offerings of help seemed feeble and hollow. In Moscow, I had made seven new friends with the pain of their situation all too real. Nothing else seemed important.

In a way that was hard to explain, the time in Moscow rekindled a spark of faith within me. Spirituality, I suspected, had to do with attitudes of the heart, a way of being, our response to situations.

My beliefs had never been tested, nor my convictions challenged. Perhaps it was meeting people who were paying a harsh price for a belief that I took casually. Perhaps Moscow found me on holiday from my convictions, or maybe Moscow held up a mirror and I saw myself for the first time as I really was and not the façade that I had constructed of someone adrift, gaining comfort from inconsequential concerns, fooling others, but ultimately fooling only myself.

I didn't understand nor did I want to explain why I was feeling the way I did. I just wanted to hold onto that moment and to be changed by its power. If I was searching for a cause, I didn't know it. In a curious way, I felt like an explorer who had wandered far off course and suddenly recognized the trail leading out of the forest. I thought I had lost my life, and now it seemed as though it was being returned to me.

But what would I do? What could I do? I had no idea.

CHAPTER 7

Campaign to Release the Siberian Seven

Fighting for Freedom, 1981–83

Moscow had been a turbulent experience but there was no time to think. The media welcomed the first images of the Siberians in three years, and the press conference that had been planned for my return from Moscow was packed. Reporters from television, radio, and the nationals were all there. Even my friend, Robert Shelton, who had moved from New York to Brighton, sat at the back, observing the scene. "This is quite a story," he remarked, giving me a hug.

Peter Meadows' latest idea was a winner: a live telephone link to the Siberians in Moscow. The Seven had recently been allowed one telephone call a month and we decided to invite the media to listen in as television cameras in London recorded our conversation. We knew the Americans would be furious but the Seven agreed that it was a risk worth taking.

Peter Sissons reported the event on ITV's lunchtime news; BBC's *Newsnight* devoted eight minutes to the campaign's launch; the *Daily Mail* headlined, "The People the West Forgot", and radio stations across the UK broadcast extracts from the telephone call.

That Saturday, the media coverage was outstanding, as BBC cameras covered our rally at Trafalgar Square attended by over

3,000 people and the subsequent march to the Soviet Embassy in Kensington.

The Siberian Seven's third anniversary on 27 June 1981 may have been dismal in Moscow but in London and beyond, they were making television news for the first time ever.

The campaign's launch had been successful, concluding the terms of my part-time "assignment". But I couldn't turn away now. The Siberians were people I cared about. They were in trouble, and I felt I had to do everything to help them. It was simply a commitment to a group of friends.

* * *

The campaign captured the imagination of people across the UK. For Peter Vashchenko's birthday in October we decorated a lorry with a large colourful cardboard cake, balloons, and streamers; girls in bright Russian-style costumes handed out real cake with a party invitation explaining why Peter couldn't attend his own birthday celebrations. It looked stunning. Television cameras recorded one of the "party girls", Joan Edgar, with me as we handed cake to obliging newspaper editors along Fleet Street. The colourful birthday float stopped at Downing Street and the Houses of Parliament. Everyone accepted a piece of cake. Only the Soviet ambassador wouldn't come to our party. At the Soviet Embassy's gates, the media were on hand to record his refusal.

The coverage was tremendous and everyone left the event on a high. But I was in for a shock when I got home to Abbey Wood. My front door had been smashed in and there were pieces of glass in the hallway; one piece had cut the ear of Durango Rolling Thunder. The neighbours had heard a disturbance but it remained an unsolved mystery.

* * *

My first meeting at the Foreign Office (FO) was instructive, as three diplomats welcomed me with coffee and smiles. First, I was told that our campaign had been the most successful of its kind, based on the number of letters they had received. Then they asked me to get our supporters to stop writing to the FO as there was nothing they could do. Taken in by their apparent affability, I expressed concern over US attitudes. One FO official erupted in fury. He slammed the table and yelled, "Don't you think the Americans are doing everything they can for these people?"

I was overwhelmed by my first encounter in Whitehall and couldn't muster much of a response. The diplomats patted me on the back, told me that I was doing a great job, and ushered me into the courtyard at King Charles Street.

There was a breeze outside and I found myself walking down Whitehall, getting angrier by the minute. I was determined not to be intimidated again by politicians and diplomats or taken in by the curious code that they used to communicate.

David Alton MP, the first MP we contacted, did what he could but it was evident that Britain would not get involved. It was for the Americans and Russians to resolve. It was SEP – Someone Else's Problem.

After returning from Moscow, I wrote hundreds of letters asking for help. Anyone. Anywhere. It was like putting a message in a bottle and sailing it out with a prayer.

Soon after my meeting at the Foreign Office, Betsy Ramsey telephoned from Stockholm with the news that a prominent Swedish MP, Tore Nilsson, had agreed to help but wanted more information. It was a slender lead but I grabbed it and flew to Stockholm for a series of meetings in the ornate parliamentary building.

If the campaign had a strategic turning point, this was to be the first bend in the road. Within days, nine MPs sent Russian President Leonid Brezhnev a message: Sweden had offered asylum to the Siberian Seven. This was a strategic development because it offered the Soviets a way out. It also showed the Americans that their policy of intimidation had failed and that they could no longer resolve the issue behind closed doors. It was the best news that we could have hoped for, but we were forced to keep the initiative secret as the success of Sweden's offer depended on its confidentiality.

Have a heart, Mr Brezhnev

Lida Vashchenko started a hunger strike in December 1981. The international media turned the personal drama into headline news, and television crews descended on our one-room campaign office in South Wimbledon.

Lady Coggan, the wife of the former Archbishop of Canterbury, agreed to launch our latest appeal ("Have a heart, Mr Brezhnev – Let these families go") and the media gave her generous coverage, but when I telephoned Lyuba in Moscow, she was despondent.

"Well, that's good," Lyuba replied solemnly, "but go and see Haig and Gromyko. They're meeting in four days in Geneva."

Her response left me depressed and exhausted. I had spent every single day of the last seven months working on their campaign and a great effort had gone into organizing Lady Coggan's successful press conference. How could we reach the US and Soviet foreign ministers in the next few days?

Supporters called from around the country to say that radio stations were plugging Lady Coggan's appeal, but when they asked what could be done, all I could mutter in frustration was "Just pray."

The telephone rang again. The caller, with a strong Scottish accent, introduced himself as George Robertson, a Labour MP. He said, "You wrote to Michael Foot and he's asked me to assure you of the Labour Party's support for your campaign. Is there anything we can do?"

"The only thing you can do is take up the case with Haig and Gromyko when they meet in Geneva," I said dismissively, repeating what I had heard Lyuba say to me just thirty minutes earlier. I was abrasive, bordering on rudeness, my frustration seeping through every word I heard myself speak. Somehow George stayed on the line.

The idea was impossible but I tossed it out. To my surprise he quizzed me further and agreed that the summit was a good opportunity to gain international coverage for the case.

I felt the exhaustion leave my body. The man on the telephone that I was insulting was the Labour Party's foreign affairs spokesman. He didn't share my pessimism; in fact, he thought this impossible idea was achievable.

Without thinking, I heard myself say, "George, could you go to Geneva for us?"

"I've got meetings coming up but I don't think there's anything I couldn't switch," George replied. "I'll need to be briefed. Could we meet in the next hour?"

George delivered a tour-de-force performance in Geneva. He grabbed every opportunity that presented itself with the international media and the politicians. The superpowers were given a resounding message in Geneva. Britain had forced the case of the Siberian Seven onto the agenda. I knew that Haig and Gromyko weren't going to interrupt their summit to order the release of the Siberians, but the process that had started in Sweden had taken a giant leap forward in Geneva.

* * *

The lead news story on all the BBC TV bulletins on Saturday 30 January 1982, beating even the Falklands War to the top slot, reported that Lida Vashchenko was being hospitalized in Moscow, following her hunger strike. In time, she was allowed to return home to Siberia, where she joined her eleven siblings, including her brother John who was assaulted at the embassy gates on their first day in 1978.

The media regularly visited the campaign's office in Wimbledon but a lack of funds threatened to close us down. When the bank froze our account, Joan Edgar, now our only full-time worker, helped me pack our materials into cardboard boxes and we moved everything from *Buzz* magazine's Wimbledon office into my home in Abbey Wood. Campaign files lay next to my Elvis vinyls.

Joan Baez was the first celebrity to add her name to a letter to *The Times* in support of the Siberians, and Humanitas, her human rights group, donated a generous amount to us following one of her London concerts. This kept us going for a few months. John Cleese, Tom Stoppard, James Fox, Judi Dench, and Glenda Jackson were among the celebrities who sent messages. When we asked Cliff Richard to sign a petition, he replied, "Their plight certainly underlies how easy we Christians have it. The signing of my name seems pathetic when one considers the suffering involved, but if it helps, here it is." The chess grandmaster, Viktor Korchnoi, pulled out of a meeting at the last moment. His excuse was simply that his family had permission to leave Russia. His telegram read, "Thanks for understanding the situation. Next time you can count on me."

Mrs Margaret Thatcher's second letter in 1982 gave us a boost. It declared that Britain would offer asylum to the Siberian Seven, essentially repeating the offer Sweden had made over a year ago. We immediately cranked out copies of the Prime Minister's message to our supporters. The letter was a kind of trophy and I wanted everyone to share in its triumph.

But not everyone welcomed her message with appropriate reverence. When the letter was left on the photocopier, Durango Rolling Thunder left muddy footprints on the page as he scrambled across the living room one rainy afternoon.

All the major moves had been played. We had done everything we could. Now we had to maintain the pressure. Who could predict what would happen next?

Freedom

I always believed it would happen, but when it happened I couldn't believe it. In April 1983, the US Consul telephoned from Moscow: "Lida's going to be released! She's coming out tomorrow."

It was electrifying news, and even the American official sounded shaken. "Can you meet her in Austria and co-ordinate her arrival?"

In Vienna, Felix Bloch, the acting US ambassador, was jovial and operated more like an accomplice than a diplomat. We set off for the airport in the embassy's limousine but parted before we reached the terminal building. "Just tell me what you want and we'll arrange it," he said conspiratorially. "But we can't be directly involved."

Lida arrived on a smoky April evening. Despite the secrecy, the story had leaked out to the international media, and a pack of reporters stalked the exits of Vienna's crowded terminal searching for signs of their prey. Mysteriously, airport security located me in the busy terminal building and I was ushered into a small, airless room.

And there she was, Lida Vashchenko, frail, fragile, even tinier than I had recalled, fired with an inner strength, the first step in the fulfilment of her family's 22-year-old dream. As we stepped out of the airport's security area, the media swooped: television cameras rolling, flash bulbs blazing, reporters firing questions. Everyone was desperate to hear the first words from the girl who had forced the hand of the superpowers to release her.

The media deluged our hotel as the intrigue intensified. Even White House representatives flew in to meet with us. Lida's mood swings matched her decisions, which changed by the hour. One American official became agitated. "She's got to go to Israel. Get her on the first flight. That's all," he told me.

I was determined that Lida should make her own decisions. She said she would pray about the decision and agreed within an hour.

The Americans were delighted but relentless. They forced the Israelis to open their embassy minutes after sabbath ended to process our visas and within hours, Lida, Ray Barnett, another activist, and I were on Israeli soil.

The next few weeks in Israel were turbulent as every new day produced another twist. News from Siberia dictated Lida's moods while I insisted she kept a low profile to avoid upsetting the Russians. It was seductive living on room service, mixing with the "movers and shakers", and "helping Lida". But was this what I wanted to do with my life? I walked along Tel Aviv's stony beach and within half an hour I knew what I had to do.

Lida had to decide herself how she used her freedom. She was comfortable with Ray Barnett, and I handed in my notice as a "minder". Beyond that, the Siberians had recently left the American Embassy in Moscow and had returned to Chernogorsk. I had a campaign to run. Lida didn't object and within twenty-four hours I was booked on an early morning flight back to London.

Back in Abbey Wood, Joan had kept the office running and Piccadilly Radio's Bryce Cooke travelled down from Cheadle Hume to help with communication. The campaign continued as though nothing had happened, but Lida's release had fired us with hope.

* * *

With theatrical precision, the Soviets released the Vashchenko family on 27 June 1983, five years to the exact day that their ordeal in the embassy had begun. Fifty-five days after Lida's release, we assembled in Vienna for an extraordinary reunion.

The media frenzy intensified as tempers flared but the correspondents from *Time* and *Newsweek* took charge. Everyone got their story and the Siberian Seven made the front page of newspapers around the world.

One month later, the scene was re-enacted, one last time. Twenty-one-year-old Timothy, his new bride, Tatiana, and thirteen members of the Chmykhalov family touched down briefly in Vienna en route to America. Again, tears of relief and joy, and abundant thanks to God.

But why were they freed? Whatever top-level deal had been fixed between the superpowers behind closed doors, without the dynamic combination of prayer, campaigning, political pressure, and publicity, it's likely that these two Siberian families would have remained at the bottom of the "fix-it" list.

The Siberians were convinced that their faith was the key and I wasn't going to argue. I caught a glimpse of that faith as Moscow caught me adrift, holidaying from my commitments. The campaign and encounters in Moscow had altered the direction of my life.

The players
The campaign lasted three years and many of the characters had stories to tell:

- The Vashchenko family stayed briefly in Israel and then moved to America.
- The Chmykhalovs settled around California.
- Peter Meadows went on to other exploits, including the setting up of London's Premier Radio.
- David Alton's commitment never wavered. After eighteen years as MP for Liverpool (Penny Lane and Strawberry Fields were in his constituency, he reminded me recently), he was honoured as Lord Alton of Liverpool.
- George Robertson moved to the House of Lords and headed up the NATO Alliance. When George was accused of helping the KGB, I was pleased to provide a statement for his libel case documenting George's support for the Siberian Seven.
- Felix Bloch, the friendly diplomat in Austria, hit the headlines in the US when he was accused of spying for Russia.

CHAPTER 8

Jailhouse Rock

Valeri Barinov's Trumpet Call, *1981–87*

The Siberian Seven Campaign had been successful – the Seven and their families were free. I was out of a job. The campaign had its way of extending its circle. I had signed up for three and a half days a week, strictly for two months. Joan Edgar joined for six weeks in 1982, to help organize Human Wrongs Day. She was a northern girl from Cheshire and had become my best friend. She would always do the right thing, even when no one was watching. All my money had been spent on the campaign. I had no savings in the bank to pay the mortgage. My job prospects were dismal. Joan must have been full of faith. She was also in love.

When the campaign started three years earlier, no one could have predicted that it would have ended for Joan and me, on 7 January 1984, with Timothy Chmykhalov as the best man at our wedding.

Peter Meadows' wedding gift was a holiday that became our honeymoon, and an unexpected donation at a meeting arranged by Gerald Coates, from the Cobham Fellowship in Surrey, covered our wedding expenses. It was a relief not to start married life with a debt.

At the meeting, Gerald remarked, "Find out who your friends are." Joan and I were struck by his comment as we'd been discussing this in the car on the journey to Cobham. We knew a lot of people, but wondered how many of them were real friends? We felt isolated in Abbey Wood and had intended to move, so explored the possibility of living in Cobham where people from the church had expressed interest in our work. But Cobham was an expensive village and there were few properties we could afford.

On 27 February 1985, Jessica was born at Queen Mary's Hospital, Sidcup, South London, and I was mesmerized as I held her in my arms for the first time. I felt my life change and we developed a bond that was stronger than anything I had known or experienced.

That same year a two-bedroomed semi-detached house in Cobham became available. It was an ex-council property and much cheaper so we put in an offer that was accepted. One bedroom was set up as an office with our files and leaflets spread across the living room. Jessica's toys frequently mingled with our campaigning materials. She acquired my "Free Nelson Mandela" badge which she took to "show and tell" at the local playgroup. Over time, the office took over all the available space in our home, with my Elvis memorabilia, *Rolling Stone* magazines and unpublished Dylan manuscript relegated to archive boxes in the garage and loft. When Jessica needed a room of her own, we moved her into our bedroom. It meant that Joan and I slept on the living room floor and had to roll up our sleeping bags before starting work each day, and in time before the volunteers arrived.

Although the Siberian Seven campaign was over, we'd been drawn into other appeals for help. The first was from one of the Siberians themselves. On the day that Timothy Chmykhalov and his family arrived in the West in July 1983 he introduced me to Tatiana, the charming Siberian girl he had married before they left Russia. In Vienna, he asked, "Tatiana's family have problems at home in Siberia. We want them to join us in the West but don't know what to do. Will you help us?"

We were tired from the non-stop three-year campaign, but Timothy had become a friend so we couldn't refuse. We succeeded in getting Tatiana's sisters and mother out of Russia but, as refugees, they got stuck in Rome. Tatiana's mother told us that criminal gangs who controlled the underworld in the city seemed to have access to refugee accommodation where families like theirs had been housed, and that she was worried that Tatiana's youngest sister would be picked up and become one of their victims. The authorities seemed to turn a blind eye to the gangs and there were rumours of girls disappearing and being trafficked across Europe.

Our supporters were fired up by the success of the Siberian Seven campaign and responded with financial gifts to help Tatiana's family. This enabled us to take action: we investigated the situation in Rome and obtained safe accommodation for the family. Eventually we secured a safe passage out of Italy in 1984, and there was an emotional reunion with Timothy and the rest of the family in America. It was exhilarating being able to help in such a direct, practical way and to know that things could change so dramatically.

But life behind the scenes was a struggle, mainly for Joan, who was helping in the office, running our home, and faced with paying for the shopping each week with meagre resources coming in. Dirk Jan Groot, of Dorcas Aid in Holland, cajoled a Dutch television company to appoint me as their London correspondent and it paid some of our expenses for the month. It worked for a while, but I wasn't able to keep this up as the requests for our help increased. Later, we were supported by Gerald Coates's organization and the Cobham Fellowship. Although this didn't cover our expenses, we felt it right that donations sent to us should only be used for direct campaign costs and not for our salary.

In Moscow everything that I believed had been put to the test. The question that I carried with me was simply this: what did I want to do with my life? The question answered itself with news from Leningrad that was set to become our next major campaign.

Turning smuggler

In 1981, while planning another visit to the Siberian Seven, friends from the Ichthus Fellowship in South London asked if I would play postman and carry a gift for someone in Leningrad.

"Sure," I said, and promptly forgot about it.

When it arrived, I was shocked to see a bright red electric guitar. "How will I get this through customs without creating suspicion?" I enquired. The reply came: "We'll pray for you."

Russian customs officials had a simple rule. Everyone was prey. At Moscow's Sheremetyevo Airport, our queue moved the slowest. As we inched nearer the front, I realized the official checking our line was scrutinizing everyone's luggage with military precision. On the counter beside him was seized contraband: books, tapes, clothes. A friend told me that he had witnessed an incident when one customs officer held up a book to his colleague and said in Russian, "Do you want to read this?" When the official nodded, the book was seized. There was no appeal.

I was sure that the guitar would be confiscated. With one passenger in front of me, my carefully rehearsed explanations sounded ludicrous. My anxiety level was high and rising.

I was concentrating so intently that I hadn't noticed that a new counter had opened up alongside us to reduce the lengthy queue, and the customs officer assigned to the post was pointing directly at me. I stumbled across to the new line. I could hear several other passengers move swiftly behind me.

The moment had come. I held up my battered suitcase and the guitar case. The customs official looked in his teens and grinned when he saw the guitar. "Beatles? You like Beatles?"

"Yes," I answered nervously. "I like the Beatles."

"Beatles are good," he said enthusiastically.

He proceeded to name his favourite Beatles songs. I quickly agreed that they were also my favourites.

He raised his eyebrows when I told him I was visiting Russia on holiday. "I want go Liverpool for holiday," he said wistfully. "Beatles," he contributed, as explanation. We both nodded.

After a few perfunctory questions, he handed me back my passport, we shook hands, and I was waved through. I walked quickly through the customs hall and didn't look back. The guitar was in. The gift was for Valeri Barinov.

Travelling beyond Leningrad's city limits, I found my way to his apartment. Valeri had a raw energy and recklessness and spoke of his faith in a way that stirred me.

He told me that he was raised in a state orphanage and joined the army as a teenager. In his own words, he was a rebel: "I was a bad man. I would get drunk all the time, fight with people."

Contemplating suicide, the ringing of a cathedral bell caused him to pull back, and he eventually became a Christian believer. Valeri was known among Leningrad's street people and spoke fearlessly at communist youth clubs, sharing his faith between his version of popular rock songs. He should have been awarded a gold record for endeavour. Instead the Russians rewarded him with a criminal record.

Weeks after my visit Valeri sent me a message asking for a synthesizer; at the same time, we were given a generous gift and I decided to use the money on Valeri's request. This time I called my friends in Ichthus and asked them to carry the musical instrument and, again, it slipped past customs officers.

Valeri had composed *Trumpet Call*, a rock musical similar to *Jesus Christ Superstar* and the secret recording had been meticulously planned for months. Just hours later and the synthesizer wouldn't have got there in time to be used on the recording.

The BBC World Service broadcast *Trumpet Call* in Russian, and it caused a sensation, turning Valeri into a local hero. Soviet censors jammed further broadcasts.

Later when BBC technicians went on strike, the censors relaxed their vigilance. Perhaps the Russian guardians of the mind had gone out for a smoke, as no one seemed to notice that the music filling the uncensored airwaves was Valeri's trumpet call to the world.

But Valeri's music was proving dangerous, and when he was arrested in 1983, we recognized the fingerprints of the KGB. In October of that year, Valeri was detained in a psychiatric hospital for a few weeks. His wife, Tanya, was told, "Your husband's views on religion differ so much from those of ordinary citizens that he needs psychiatric treatment." He was released but arrested in 1984 for trying to "escape" and held in Leningrad's KGB headquarters as a high-risk prisoner. Later that year he was sentenced to several years' imprisonment. News from inside Valeri's labour camp was sparse but alarming, and following reports that he had suffered a heart attack, we intensified our campaign. David Alton visited his family with practical help. Tapes of *Trumpet Call* were smuggled out of Russia, and with support from Ichthus, Keston College, Word Records, and others, we released the secret recordings.

We thought publicity and pressure were our best weapons and we got his story covered in *The Sun*, *The Times*, and *New Musical Express*; David Alton enlisted the support of both Neil Kinnock and David Steel, the leaders of the Labour and Liberal Parties. When ITV News interviewed me, Valeri's music was broadcast on television for the first time.

We wanted Neil Kinnock to intervene during his visit to Moscow in 1984, but Joan didn't know which hotel the Labour leader was staying in so directed our communication to the British Embassy with a hope and a prayer that they would pass it on.

The telegram cost £30. With our finances at breaking point we hesitated about spending the money but went ahead. That weekend *The Sunday Times* carried Kinnock's visit on its front page and our appeal for Valeri was right there. In fact, Mr Kinnock had been at the British Embassy, and our message had been placed in his hands while he was being interviewed by reporters from *The Sunday Times*.

It was the last time we would hesitate about spending our money on campaigning.

Arrest and release

A friend visited Valeri just days after his release in 1986 and told us that his eyes were alive but his body was weak from illness, a heart attack, and beatings. His home for the last two years had been a labour camp chillingly named "Blood Camp".

Valeri appealed to Mikhail Gorbachev to leave Russia and we passed a copy to Mrs Thatcher before her official visit to the Soviet Union in 1987. Valeri called me days after her departure and said that local emigration officials had asked him to obtain a formal invitation which I provided, authorized through the Foreign Office. When Leningrad officials received my documentation, they told him to pack his bags and leave in two days.

"That's great news," I told Valeri on the phone.

Valeri laughed. "Yes. But they're not going to tell me when to leave. I'll make that decision."

He spent his last weeks speaking and singing wherever he could. In October, he held an open-air concert outside an atheist museum (once a Leningrad cathedral), and the inevitable happened: Valeri was arrested.

When I reached him on the telephone I expressed sympathy to hear that they were fined fifty roubles. But Valeri laughed, "The fine was OK. If we hired a hall for a meeting, with a sound system, and everything else, it would have cost us over 300 roubles. This was only fifty roubles. It was cheap."

Valeri's arrival at Heathrow Airport was a wonderful moment captured on BBC TV News, and media coverage was high over the next few weeks.

Driving through the streets of London one night, shortly after his arrival, we cruised down London's Regent Street. It was past midnight and the brightly coloured decorative neon advertised a secularized Christmas. Valeri was enthralled and turned to me, somewhat wistfully, and said, "I can't believe this is happening. It's like a gift to us." My instinctive observation was that Valeri was a gift to us in the West.

CHAPTER 9

Proclaiming Jubilee

Parliamentarians Take Action, 1986–95

I learned two things while campaigning for the Siberian Seven and Valeri Barinov. First, that the Soviet authorities hunted and imprisoned religious believers but they could be influenced by pressure and publicity. Second, that communist Russia wasn't the only abuser of human rights.

After meeting Timothy Renton, the Foreign Office minister, in 1986, about a Romanian prisoner, David Alton and I were having coffee in Parliament when I mentioned that I'd just heard that the Turkish government had imposed a ban on the Bible. Later that evening, David's researcher, David Campanale, telephoned. "David Steel has an official meeting with Turgut Ozal, Turkey's Prime Minister. How quickly can you get us a report about the ban?"

We worked around the clock to document the incident and our report was handed to the Liberal Party leader on his way to meet the Prime Minister of Turkey. After completing official business with Mr Ozal, Mr Steel raised the Bible ban in the context of censorship and press freedoms.

Mr Ozal replied, "I'll look into it."

True to his word, he did, and months later, the Turkish Ministry of the Interior published an official decree formally lifting the ban on the Bible.

In 1986, we still operated as the "Siberian Seven Committee", but the network of friends that was involved with us as an unofficial board insisted that I come up with a new name. I chose "Jubilee Campaign" because it reflected the Jewish idea of justice. It was taken from the Old Testament teaching that every fifty years there should be a Year of Jubilee when prisoners and slaves were pardoned, debts were forgiven, and property returned to their owners – a redistribution of wealth. I saw justice in action as the defining principle of our mission and the work I wanted to do.

That year, a friend at church put up the money for the salary of our first worker and Rosie McLaughlin joined us full time. Rosie started work at our home and brought with her more volunteers, and before long we were a houseful. The same friend invited us to move the office from our home into his. With Joan pregnant with our second child, we didn't hesitate.

As the global scale of religious persecution became clearer to us, David Alton wanted to use his influence as a Member of Parliament to help. "Let's ask MPs to take action for individual cases and 'adopt' them," he enthused at a meeting early in January 1987, and set a date in February when Jubilee Campaign would be launched in Parliament's aptly titled Jubilee Room. Our first project was David's deceptively simple idea of inviting MPs to "adopt" prisoners of faith.

With only a few weeks before the launch, Rosie squeezed extra hours out of the day to mobilize her army of volunteers to prepare "prisoner case files" and to select a sumptuous array of international delicacies for the event. Parliamentary rules prohibited food being taken into the rooms but we found a creative way through the bureaucratic maze. We decided not to request permission. If we didn't ask, they couldn't refuse.

I didn't know how MPs would respond but David's energy and commitment propelled us forward. Without him alongside, I don't know how far we would have got. The launch was well attended and halfway through a courier arrived from Downing

Street with an endorsement from the Prime Minister. Meanwhile, word quickly spread in the House of Commons that you could sample a rare Ukrainian beer, an unusual selection of fresh fruit, and ethnic nibbles in the Jubilee Room. More importantly, over thirty MPs "adopted" prisoners of faith on the spot and the number doubled within days.

There was success at home as well. One month after Jubilee Campaign was launched in Parliament, Joan went into labour and we headed straight for Epsom Hospital. The nursing staff considered Joan to be so calm that they wanted to send her home. "I'm not leaving," she insisted. "I'm having a baby!" Joan was right of course and Rachel was born late in the afternoon of 10 March. I can still remember the surge of joy that overwhelmed me. Joan noticed that I'd been wearing the same shirt when Jessica was born. I never wore it again but had it washed, ironed, and ready in case we ever needed it in the future.

* * *

Our team also increased as Richard Warnes and Howard Taylor raised their own salaries and joined Rosie and me in our friend's home/office, alongside several volunteers whom Rosie recruited. MPs took action, and the diplomatic salvos fired from within Parliament over the next few months hit targets all across the globe.

David Alton's idea of an "adoption" programme in Parliament had been a remarkable success, and over 150 MPs joined us to take up cases of prisoners of faith from countries as politically different as South Africa, Burma, China, Egypt, Vietnam, Nepal, Sudan, Iran, Guatemala, the Soviet Union, and Eastern Europe. The campaigning activity of the MPs was reported by national and local news, alerting their constituents that they were tackling the important issues of human rights and religious persecution. It would take another book to recount these achievements. Only a few are reported here.

Cyprus, 1988

In August 1988, we were asked to take up the case of a young man imprisoned in Nicosia, Cyprus. Erdinc Ucjac, a Kurd of Turkish origin, had been arrested with two others from the student group Youth with a Mission, but when both were released, he was held without charge for several months. When the prosecutor eventually pressed charges, Erdinc's defence lawyers weren't permitted to see any details. We sent the case to Cyril Townsend, one of the MPs who agreed to join our adoption programme.

Mr Townsend telephoned us the following day. "I can't believe this. Surely there must be a stronger case against him than the details you have sent me?" he said, genuinely baffled.

Richard Warnes, our parliamentary officer, provided verification and Mr Townsend was reassured. He said, "I am hopeful that I can do something. I am currently Chairman of the British–Cyprus Commonwealth Parliamentary Association. If I can't help, then who can?"

As a direct result of Mr Townsend's intervention, Erdinc was released from prison and allowed to leave Cyprus. Richard was a former army officer with an impressive and colourful vocabulary but the timing of this encounter left him speechless. Out of 651 MPs in Parliament, we had been directed to the only one who could make a difference.

Nepal, 1989

I knew Nepalese people to be gentle and friendly, and was disturbed at the grim reports about the attacks against Christians and churches in Nepal, the world's only Hindu kingdom. The worst incident was that a father had been arrested for arranging a religious burial for his child.

Some foreign groups were concerned that campaigning would affect their status, but when the head of the Nepalese Bible Society, on behalf of local church leaders, personally contacted us for help, we launched a campaign to seek changes in the law.

I asked my friend Charles Mendies in Nepal to help us document the issue, and our report of two decades of persecution from 1970 to 1988 was published at a hearing in Parliament hosted by David Alton. Charles spoke at the meeting and said, "Despite this intense persecution, the indigenous church remained strong." In 1960, there were virtually no baptized believers in Nepal, but the number had grown to 25,000 people by 1990. Nepal was a tolerant country but extremists were driving the attacks.

We knew Charles was taking a risk. Charles had been arrested for "preaching", and an article about him in the Gideons' magazine was used as evidence of his crime. He had visited us in the UK while on bail but when he returned to Nepal he was sentenced to 1,000 days in jail.

I was worried that our involvement might have contributed to his imprisonment, and in 1990 I flew to Nepal to offer support to his family.

Kathmandu is a dazzling, exotic city set amid the awesome splendour of the spectacular Himalayan mountain range. Samantha Fox posters and *Rambo* videos in the bazaar were visual reminders that tourism and Western influences had made inroads into this once-hidden, mysterious land. During the sixties, Kathmandu became a mystical haven on the hippie trail. It was a focal point of pilgrimage for rambling and disconnected youth who trekked up the mountain in search of answers to the meaning of life. In the sixties, I had made the journey from India to Nepal by road with a friend from the student group OM. The path literally wound up the mountain, granting us an incredible view of the land below, and glimpses, covered in mist, of the highest point on earth. The bus drivers were tigerish as they pushed their vehicles forward on slim, winding tracks up the mountain. It was a tumultuous ride, one that I have never forgotten, etched on my memory by sheer terror and incredible beauty.

Charles's wife, Susan, combined resilience and determination with a clear sense of responsibility and realism. She told me, "I was shocked when the police arrested Charles. We could have escaped, but why should we? We are Nepali and proud of our land, our home. If this is the price we must pay for being true to our faith, then so be it. Charles and I knew it would be hard but we are prepared to be apart for the next three years."

The day after I arrived in the hilltop kingdom, Susan took me to Central Jail, about fifteen minutes away from their home. The jail held 700 prisoners and Charles shared a cell with seventeen others. Victor, a Russian, was on a murder charge. Michael, from Reading, had been nabbed for dealing drugs.

Prisoners met their families at one of the jail's gates, under the close supervision of armed guards. Behind cold steel bars, the prisoners peered through padlocked gates. Five feet away, we huddled together in the street along with other prison visitors, straining for a better view.

Seven prisoners stood shoulder to shoulder inside the jail, each one yelling messages to the outside world. Mothers and wives, fathers and sons, shouted back their replies, sometimes simultaneously. Through prison bars, Charles sounded resolute: "I could be in prison for three years. It's in God's hands."

His young son Daniel was perched in my arms listening intently, but when it was time to leave, he moved towards the prison gates as Charles crouched down with outstretched arms. But the guard stepped in. "No!" he said. No physical contact was permitted. Little Daniel extended his arm and for a precarious moment the orders were defied as their fingers touched. The crowd appeared to have hushed, observing this human drama being enacted, for each one in Central Jail understood the significance of this embrace between father and son.

But it was not to be, and Daniel stood in the dusty street, waving goodbye to Papa.

The UN, 1990

Susan helped me slip into another jail to visit Pastor Tir Bahadur Dewan, aged seventy-eight, who had started the first Nepali church in the country. Two vanloads of police raided his church at Bhaktapur, and seized the entire congregation of thirty-nine people. Many were beaten badly as police ransacked the church. When we visited the area, local people were dismayed at the way police manhandled the elderly preacher and some of the women.

David Armstrong, from the organization Send the Vision, filmed wherever appropriate, and BBC Television used the footage, while *The Times* covered the story.

I pressed the Nepalese cases in Whitehall and was told that the issue was on the agenda during official talks with Nepal's Foreign Minister. It was an indication of the impact campaigning can make. I wanted to get the United Nations involved and we had been circulating a petition calling on them to take action but didn't know what to do next.

As I was leaving our office in Richmond, I was reminded of a 5 p.m. meeting with a young American law student. I suspected that this was another earnest but naïve person who had the answer to the world's problems and wanted to take my time discussing their impractical theories for the next few hours. Before I could foist the meeting onto someone else, our guest was ushered into our cramped office. I was trapped.

Ann Buwalda perched on the edge of a table and said, "I've been studying the UN legal system and am looking for a case study to take up. Can you help or do you know someone who can?"

I didn't reply but reached to the side of my desk, clutched a bundle of our UN petitions and shoved them over to her.

Over the next month, Ann co-ordinated the action and we invited John Smith (sometimes called a biker and blues preacher) from Australia to speak for us about the Nepal campaign at the UN's Human Rights Commission in Geneva. Ann returned to

Washington and drummed-up support on Capitol Hill, opening up another portal for the campaign.

In the summer of 1990, the government announced an amnesty, and both Tir Bahadur Dewan and Charles Mendies were released. The elderly pastor needed urgent medical treatment and we were able to pay for his operation. There were whoops and cheers when Charles Mendies came on the phone just hours after he was freed. He said, "I received 2,674 letters and cards from Britain. Ninety per cent of these were people directly involved in your campaign for my release. Fantastic! It was a fantastic encouragement to know that there were people praying for me and taking action."

Pakistan, 1993–95

In Pakistan, the attacks against the Christian minority were relentless over several years. Many of the assaults were from extremists while personal grudges and disputes appeared to be the motive for other complaints. In 1993, Fazul-ul-Haq, an Islamic cleric in Pakistan, filed a complaint of blasphemy against eleven-year-old Salamat Masih and two others, Rehmat Masih and Manzoor Masih. The slim, elderly cleric claimed that the trio had scribbled blasphemous words on the wall of his mosque in Gujranwala, the fifth largest industrial city in Pakistan. Islamic sharia law ruled that all three could be convicted on the word of a single witness. The penalty was death by hanging, but I was sceptical that any court would order a child to be executed. The boy was illiterate and only learned to write his name in prison.

The Foreign Office was unaware of the incident when we contacted them but instructed its embassy to take up the case and maintained pressure from that moment on. In Washington, Ann organized an appeal by politicians Frank Wolf, Tom Lantos, Tony Hall, and Christopher Smith.

I contacted our friends at the *Sunday Express* and they were the first to report the story (in December 1993). For once the tabloid-newspaper headline seemed appropriate: "Graffiti Boy Faces Hangman". One year later, we raised Salamat's case by name at the United Nations, but tragedy struck in April 1994.

After returning from a court appearance, the three defendants were standing at a bus stop outside the court buildings on a teeming street in Lahore. Hit men on motorbikes cruised by and opened fire. The sudden violence took everyone by surprise as the thunder of gunfire sent everyone running for cover.

Salamat was hit in the hand but the others with him took the force of the assassins' guns. Manzoor Masih died instantly, his body riddled with twelve bullets. He left a widow with ten children. Rehmat Masih was seriously wounded, and a church leader with them was shot in the face.

Under pressure from fundamentalists, their lawyer dropped their case. I was relieved when Asma Jahangir, Pakistan's best-known human rights advocate, agreed to defend them. I had visited Asma in Pakistan and knew she was outstandingly courageous and a brilliant lawyer.

Asma told me about the incident: "I was in a shop nearby when my office rang me on my mobile phone and told me that there had been a shooting."

She went directly to the local hospital, and as she was talking to one of the victims, he scribbled a note and surreptitiously passed it to her. The note read, "The man in blue behind you is the shooter." Asma said, "I gasped in astonishment and turned around. My shocked reaction prompted the assassin to turn and flee."

The shooting sent shockwaves through the local community, but three months later, the fury of the fundamentalists erupted in a weekend of frenzy. At a Saturday afternoon rally (in July 1994) an extremist called Maulana Darkhwasti created a furore by offering a 1-million rupee reward (about £20,000) to anyone who assassinated Pakistan's Minister of Law, Mr Syed Iqbal Haider (nicknamed "Pakistan's Salman Rushdie"). He had enraged the extremists after an interview he'd given to the BBC in London had been broadcast in Pakistan. The day before the interview, Mr Haider told David Alton and our parliamentary officer, Wilfred Wong (who had raised Salamat's case and others), that amendments to the blasphemy law were being considered.

On the day of the rally, stickers appeared on buses and buildings throughout Lahore calling for the death of Asma Jahangir. No one could explain how the two coloured stickers came to be distributed with that morning's edition of the English language newspaper, *The Dawn*.

Mrs Jahangir told me, "The stickers say that I am the worst of all blasphemers. It is the duty of all Muslims to 'find her and kill her'."

Encouraged by her friends, Asma Jahangir appointed a bodyguard armed with a Kalashnikov rifle who followed her everywhere, including into the courtroom, as she conducted Salamat's defence.

On 9 February 1995, the judge finally delivered the verdict that everyone feared: death by hanging. One week later, on 16 February, a violent demonstration at Lahore's high court insisted – loudly – that Asma Jahangir's name should be added to the death list. Asma's car was attacked by the mob but her driver was whisked to safety.

"My friends said, 'We saved your driver but couldn't save your car'," Asma joked with me when relating the incident. Protected by her personal bodyguard, she left the court under police escort.

Travelling with Asma (and bodyguard) in Pakistan, I found myself continually on edge, yet she maintained a sense of calm and normality. It was this determination to remain unbowed that afforded her the moral authority over her tormentors.

An appeal against Salamat's judgment was lodged in the high court, but on 23 February 1995 the original charge of blasphemy was withdrawn on Salamat and the other person charged with him (Rehmat Masih). I was with Asma Jahangir on the same day that the case collapsed. We hoped that our lobbying had played a part in the decision but she told me, "Don't start celebrating – it's not over. The extremists will want revenge and I am sure that there will be other similar cases. The blasphemy law should be changed."

Asma's courage equalled her convictions. She wasn't a Christian herself, but the Christian community remains in her debt, for she placed herself in peril by identifying so strongly with them. On one occasion when I met her, she told me, "I just learned that my office received a handwritten letter from a fanatic saying that he had been in court with a gun intending to shoot me. The letter said, 'I'm going to hunt you down till you are dead. That is my mission.'"

Asma told me that Salamat was like any fourteen-year-old boy. At times, these fantastic events seemed like an adventure to him, yet he was always aware of the risks that he faced. "When Salamat was told that the court's verdict had condemned him to death by hanging, he told me, 'I am in God's hands. I am sure that God will give us justice'," Asma said to me. "He seemed shocked yet calm, but when I put my arm around him, he was trembling."

Asma was convinced that the original graffiti incident was a trumped-up charge and that Salamat, Manzoor, and Rehmat were innocent. She was equally adamant that the fanatics would not be silent for long. Someone must pay. Asma was right, and since then, there have been several similar cases, some ending in murder.

CHAPTER 10

End of History

Turning Point in Eastern Europe, 1989–97

When Valeri Barinov visited us he always made time for our kids. He taught Jessica to somersault and Rachel, cautious at first, was eventually won over and followed him everywhere. When his wife Tanya learned that Joan was pregnant again, she cried, "A boy! Please, a boy!"

It was a joy to call her in January 1989 to give her the news that our son Luke arrived half an hour after midnight on Friday the 20th.

When Joan had told me that we had to leave immediately for the hospital because the contractions were coming fast and strong, I asked her to hold on. She looked at me as though I had gone loco. I dashed into our tiny bedroom to scramble into the shirt that I had worn when both Jessica and Rachel were born. I wasn't superstitious but somehow it felt good. There was a heavy fog that evening but we made it to Epsom Hospital without a speeding ticket.

It felt wonderful to have a son. As time passed and the bond between us grew, I felt I had reclaimed a relationship that I had lost in my childhood.

Romania, 1989

The year 1989 was to be a tumultuous one. No one could have predicted that it would be the year that empires started to crumble or that I would be caught up in some of the international dramas. In November, the shockwaves of the collapse of the Berlin Wall reverberated worldwide. A month later, the spotlight shifted to Romania.

Trouble was brewing in Timisoara. When secret police tried to evict Laszlo Tokes, the leader of the Hungarian Reformed Church, on 15 December 1989, church members blocked the entrance. Petru Dugulescu, the pastor of the Baptist Church, organized a 24-hour candlelit vigil.

The vigil continued for a second day, joined by even more people, while the unrest spread to other parts of the city. That night, armoured cars patrolled the streets, as patriotic songs banned by the communists were sung openly, and for the first time voices were raised in protest. Before dawn, secret police broke through the vigil and smashed the church door. They bundled Laszlo and Edith Tokes into an unmarked car and drove into the night.

The news of Tokes's abduction added fuel to the blazing emotions as thousands took to the streets in unprecedented scenes of protest. These extraordinary events in Timisoara captured news headlines worldwide but no one could be sure what was happening. The international media reported that there was a news blackout.

Not to us. Romania's communications may have closed down but we had a hotline to Timisoara and talked directly to our friend, Petru Dugulescu.

* * *

For four years, we had secretly taken supplies to Petru Dugulescu in Timisoara for distribution to the poor. Dorcas Aid in Holland got us started and Howard Taylor worked full time on the project. We rented vans, used church volunteers, and arranged between five and fifteen trips into the country annually. Contact was always made at night. If caught, we would have been deported, and Petru would have been arrested. But he was fearless and had already survived two assassination attempts.

Romania's President, Nicolae Ceausescu's, plan to bulldoze thousands of villages and demolish historical monuments and churches – some dating back to the thirteenth century – caused alarm, and even Prince Charles expressed concern. Meanwhile, in Timisoara, Petru's ambitious plan to build a thousand-seater church was paid for (and built) by his congregation. It was a remarkable accomplishment. Petru asked if we could rewire the building and provide its amplification and we completed the assignment covertly.

Richard Warnes took a call from the Foreign Office advising us to be cautious. Apparently, the intelligence service had picked up that the Romanians were curious about our frequent visits into their country.

Our team's reports from inside Romania were shocking, almost unbelievable. It was a criminal offence to use anything stronger than a 40-watt light bulb or to stockpile food. All typewriters were registered. Ambulances would only service adults who could work, while the elderly and children were ignored. Christians were routinely imprisoned, while Bibles were pulped and recycled into toilet paper. Each family was required to produce as many babies as possible – future workers for the state – but with severe food shortages, many were abandoned in squalid orphanages including those born with birth defects.

We were repulsed by the lucrative business deals that accompanied the honours Western countries seemed intent on bestowing on Ceausescu. The dictator stayed overnight at Buckingham Palace in June 1978 and was awarded an honorary knighthood. In *Kiss the Hand You Cannot Bite* Edward Behr observed that the Callaghan government convinced the Queen that "the importance of imminent aircraft and arms sales to Romania made such hospitality mandatory". Similarly, President

Giscard d'Estaing invited the Ceausescus to France as part of a trade deal involving Renault and the computer firm Bull.

We were in a catch-22 situation. We couldn't publicize our work without endangering Petru and others.

* * *

With the streets on fire in December 1989, it seemed there was only one telephone line left open inside Romania. And it belonged to Petru. The media deluged our one-room office in Richmond and the latest news from Romania was broadcast to the world. Petru gave us a running commentary on daily activity and sometimes media agencies called us to verify rumours they'd heard.

ITV *News at Ten* whisked me down to their London studio for an interview, and as I finished one of their reporters told me there was an urgent phone call from the office. It was Robert Day, who whispered conspiratorially, "Don't say anything but BBC TV News have a car outside. They want you to go live on TV News tonight. But they don't want you to tell ITV."

The skies turned dark on 17 December. In Bucharest, the order was given to crush the protest in Timisoara, and the Securitate (Secret Police) were ordered to open fire. With real bullets. Hundreds of demonstrators were hit; many were killed, including members of Petru's church.

The Securitate buried the dead in mass graves, but before reinforcements from Bucharest could arrive, the army switched sides on 19 December and backed the demonstrators. Ceausescu cut short a visit to Iran and returned the following day to deal with the uprising.

But time had run out for the dictator. The television cameras recorded every twist, as street fighting and sheer people power forced him to flee. With the country in upheaval, Nicolae and Elena Ceausescu escaped by helicopter. It ran out of fuel and was forced to land. The couple were picked up by a startled motorist and eventually arrested. Charged with embezzlement and genocide, the Ceasescus were taken from their improvised courtroom and executed by firing squad on Christmas Day.

In Timisoara, the news that Ceausescu's regime had fallen was greeted with tumultuous applause and palpable joy. Thousands took to the streets and gathered in the city's main promenade, Opera Square, the scene where many had fallen. When people in the crowd called for a Christian message, Petru stepped forward and led the crowd in the Lord's Prayer, as the thousands gathered in the square knelt on the ground, bowed their heads, and raised their voices together, in a moment of declared repentance and hope.

Petru's son, Christy, captured the historic event on camera. It was to become a moving tribute to the triumph of faith following decades of oppression, and an important symbolic victory as the place where Petru had stood in Opera Square was the very point where Ceausescu had regularly appeared whenever he visited Timisoara.

Later, Laszlo Tokes was released and turned to politics. In 2010 he was elected as the Vice President of the European Union.

The spark of light that had ignited change in Timisoara was to spread.

Moscow, 1990–91

While Pier Paolo Pasolini's movies shocked audiences in the West and some demanded that they should be banned, one of his films made a profound impact on a young student in Moscow's Institute of Cinematography. Alexander Ogorodnikov watched an early Pasolini film about the life of Christ and found himself drawn to the central character. As a result, Alexander joined the Orthodox Church but this didn't go unnoticed. Expelled from the film school, he was hounded when he set up a student discussion group and arrested in 1978, charged with "parasitism" – described as the catch-22 of the criminal code: the victims were prevented from getting a job, then prosecuted for not working. His "trial" followed a familiar pattern; the public benches were filled in advance by the KGB, so that his friends could not get in. Even his wife and mother were admitted only after lengthy arguments and for only part of the trial.

Alexander was imprisoned in Perm 36, one of the worst prisons in the Soviet Union and then fell victim to the Soviets' latest vicious trick. He was re-sentenced while still in prison. He smuggled a letter out of the camp to his mother. Always a gifted writer, it described the pathos and despair that defined his tortured life.

Jubilee Campaign reproduced this moving document as a poster and circulated it widely. The letter created a stir. Even Bernard Levin, *The Times*' celebrated columnist, dedicated an "op ed" feature to him.

The publicity and pressure worked. President Reagan, among others, called for his release. At a summit with Mrs Thatcher in 1987, President Gorbachev declared that Alexander was to be freed. Everyone in the human rights circle breathed a collective sigh of relief. But the cruellest deceit was the final one. Behind the scenes, a personal tragedy was awaiting him. Convinced by the KGB that Alexander would never be released and told that he would die in prison, his wife, Irina, remarried just days before prison gates opened and he walked out a free man. Unlike other dissidents, Alexander chose to stay in Russia, and we helped him set up a political party, the Christian Democratic Union.

In 1990 newspaper reports warned of food shortages in Moscow. Late one night, the phone rang and I recognized Alexander's soft, lilting voice. "People are dying," Alexander said. "Old people are facing great hardships. Can you help?"

Alexander wanted to open a food kitchen to feed the poor and destitute. Together with Dorcas Aid in Holland we produced ration books with coupons. People in the West would buy the ration books for Russians to use the coupons and these would be distributed to needy families in Moscow. The idea caught on.

The Sun newspaper covered the story, and the recently formed Movement for Christian Democracy (MCD) pledged their support. In December, David Alton arranged a meeting with Soviet Ambassador Zamyatin who guaranteed the use of an Aeroflot transport plane to fly our food supplies to Moscow.

We invited our friends from the Women's Campaign for Soviet Jewry to the meeting, and we emerged somewhat dazed. After years of campaigning outside, we had now been inside the embassy face to face with people who had been the focus of our protest.

The authorities at Stanstead Airport were fantastic, while Bill Gribbin, from MCD, kept a watchful eye on the supplies at a warehouse nearby. Several tons of food piled in, with additional donations by Milupa and United Biscuits and the first planeload with its cargo was airborne on Boxing Day. We were ecstatic. So was Alexander when we phoned him with the news.

Then the trouble started. When Alexander tried to take delivery of the food at Moscow's airport he faced a familiar refrain. No one knew anything. What food? No food was on the flight. Gatwick Airport's shipping agents, Gatwick Handling, confirmed that our food was on board. Express Service, the Soviet freight forwarding company that processed the cargo, said that the aircraft arrived fully loaded but the flight manifest made no mention of food for Moscow. Soviet authorities were adamant. There was no food on the plane.

The story hit the media and the front-page report in *The Times* on 27 December 1990 told it all: "Moscow-bound food cargo goes missing". Another headline declared "Food for Russia disappears".

With 30 tons due into the warehouse, concern was mounting that our project would be discredited and supplies would dry up. The Soviets blamed us. They told the press that our food hadn't been labelled. The food could be anywhere. How do we know?

Just hours after we read the story in *The Times*, Bill Gribbin arrived in our office with photos he had taken of the cargo being loaded onto the plane. One photo showed the sign on the box: "Moscow Aid/ Jubilee Campaign/ Immediate Clearance". Bill took the pictures straight to the newspaper's office in Wapping and the next day's headline in *The Times* stated, "Missing food aid found" with Bill's photo splashed across the front page.

The photos in the media produced a Houdini-like impact in Moscow. Suddenly our food was found. Still, the local authorities stubbornly refused to hand it over, but after David Alton telephoned the ambassador, the game was up.

In the final days of the crumbling communist empire, Moscow had become the venue for a vicious turf war. The communists clung to power, refusing to give up control of lucrative under-the-counter deals, creating trouble for the genuine liberal politicians who were trying to seize the moment. Edging nearer were the notorious mafia-like gangs, determined to claim a piece of the action. Their policy was simple: they ruled by the gun and would shoot anyone who got in the way. Alexander walked a tightrope amid this violence, making enemies along the way.

The independently run Moscow City Council signed a contract with Alexander and Jubilee Campaign and Dorcas Aid for the food kitchen to be opened near the city centre, but a local communist boss, Vladimir Michailov, realized its prime location could be financially lucrative. He launched a campaign of intimidation and local thugs disrupted the building and the plans for renovation.

Despite the threats, history was made in April 1991 when the first free food kitchen in Moscow opened its doors to the poor and elderly and several hundred people were fed. Each one through the door held a coupon from the ration book that people in Britain and Holland had purchased.

But the pressure intensified. The electricity was turned off and some food in the freezer perished. Meanwhile tyres were slashed on a vehicle that we and the MCD had donated for food distribution.

In Britain, David Alton pressed the Soviet ambassador for guarantees that Alexander would not be harmed and that alternative premises be found for the food kitchen. In Moscow, something had stirred. People like Alexander had taken the first few steps of freedom, with no one knowing where it would lead. While words like "glasnost" and "perestroika" were entering textbooks, defining a moment in history, a group of hardliners held President Gorbachev a virtual prisoner as they tried to seize power in an attempted coup in August 1991. But television cameras captured courageous protesters who shielded the Russian Parliament building with their bodies. The army were called in and the tanks rolled. The world held its breath.

At midnight, Alexander telephoned me, his voice gripped by passion and nervous tension. His words tumbled out in a free-flowing stream-of-consciousness. I realized that it was important to communicate his message to others and I scribbled as he talked:

There was an electric atmosphere among the people. I was so moved. I began to cry like a child. We were among the first to take action. We did this against the direct order of the communists. We published the latest news and stuck leaflets on the walls. Our team worked day and night in the food kitchen to prepare food for the protesters. We drove to the square in your van and were there all night, walking and talking, among the people.

It was dangerous. Bullets were flying over my head. A bullet struck the van. It was a time of extraordinary courage. I saw a woman with children in her arms block a tank with her body. We stopped several soldiers and appealed to them: "Turn back!" At 3 a.m. one morning I talked with the chief of a military unit. "Don't shoot the people; don't shed the blood of our Russian people."

When the coup crumbled, there was such joy. We knew the communist system was doomed. We knew it was dead. But now we were witnessing its collapse. It was like a miracle.

The word "glasnost" became synonymous with the changes occurring within the sprawling empire of the Soviet Union, with Mikhail Gorbachev the ringmaster. Almost single-handedly, he tried to stop the tyranny while the Western world watched in shock and awe.

There were many sceptics. The poet Irina Ratushinskaya told me that she considered her release from labour camp to be a "show". Even the CIA's billion-dollar budget hadn't predicted the fall of communism. The changes were so significant that some considered the end of history was upon us and that we were on the brink of a new phase of human society and history.

As historians were seeking iconic moments to understand the changes, many were turning to dissidents, intellectuals, artists, and people of faith for the moral authority to direct the way forward. Ironically, totalitarian regimes were undermined by individual acts of defiance, illustrating Alexander Solzhenitsyn's comment that "one word of truth outweighs the world".

Poland's Adam Michnik wrote from prison, "You score a victory not when you win power but when you remain faithful to yourself." Throughout the communist world, just attending church was an act of protest. Alexander Ogorodnikov observed, "Protest became a way of life and also a way of survival in the system of lies."

Romania, 1989

Reports from inside Romania shocked the world as television coverage exposed Ceausescu's brutality and the living hell of Romania's children abandoned in degrading orphanages.

When *The Sunday Times* reported that we were among the first to take supplies into Romania we received widespread support, including a message from Olivia Harrison, the wife of former Beatle George Harrison, who wanted to make a donation. I suggested that she visit Romania herself. She was so moved by the experience that she decided to donate more than money. She set up the Romanian Angel Appeal, drawing in the wives of the Beatles, and Elton John, and invited me to serve as a trustee of the new organization.

Some of our meetings were held in the office of Elton John's manager, Steve Brown, where original Andy Warhol paintings peered down on our conversations. George Harrison was in Los Angeles at the time and Olivia telephoned him and described all she had witnessed in the orphanages. George decided he would help and drew in Bob Dylan, Tom Petty, and Jeff Lynne (the fantastic Travelling Wilburys), and they recorded "Nobody's Child" as a charity single. He sent a cassette tape days after the recording and we sat in silence listening to the song. We just played it again and again. Within weeks other artists such as Elton John, Eric Clapton, Van Morrison, and Stevie Wonder had contributed songs and an album was rushed out with all the profits going to Romania.

Almost immediately after the fall of Ceausescu, we had set about refurbishing a few of the worst orphanages in the country and a northern businessman, Malcolm Grainge, contributed a fleet of vehicles to help with logistics in Romania. The orphanages were transformed, and when Olivia and Steve saw the photographs they immediately agreed to support the initiative. Olivia and Barbara Bach (Ringo Starr's wife) went on Radio 1 and appealed for builders, plumbers, and electricians to work on the programme and gave out our telephone number for volunteers. Overnight we'd turned into a recruitment agency as we had to interview potential workers while trying to detect the cranks and glory-hunters.

The result was remarkable, with numerous orphanages renovated by hundreds of volunteers, and our plans to see an effective programme to refurbish orphanages became a reality. Olivia's magnetism, energy, and profile ensured the issue stayed on the front page, as the *Daily Mail* carried a six-week series of articles with Jubilee Campaign's address for people to send money. The album and subsequent publicity raised over $2 million.

Changing times

This was a strategic moment for us. We had a cracking team but no one was paid a salary (Rosie had moved on after three years) and each one, like me, had raised money from friends and churches for their support.

The spin doctors would have classified us as on a "mission impossible". There was no marketing plan or brand identity. The database was just a list of names and addresses. We didn't take on campaigns and projects because there was money in the bank – there wasn't. Every pound that people gave us was spent on the work, and every time we launched a new campaign we ran the risk of going bankrupt as our passion exceeded our purse. It was a precarious way to run an organization and I realized that things could have come crashing down at any moment.

Olivia and Steve asked us to continue involvement in Romania and suggested a creative merger with their new organization (the Romanian Angel Appeal). In return, they agreed to pay our team's salary for an extended period of time. Their support gave us time to generate a fundraising plan, and after a year or so, we were able to take over the funding for our own team, including me.

By then, our office had outgrown our friend's house in Cobham and we took shelter wherever space was offered. When the term of our free office in Richmond expired in early 1990, we faced becoming homeless yet again. We'd heard that the offices at Wimbledon Football Club were empty as the owner Sam Hammam was trying to sell the property, and Olivia told me that Sam had kindly agreed to allow both Jubilee Campaign and the Romanian Angel Appeal to use it until the sale went through. It was a fantastic feeling driving to the football club in Wimbledon each day, and occasionally we held meetings in the stands or strolled onto the pitch to take a break.

Olivia wanted to make a difference – and she clearly did. When immersed in a complex discussion one day, she cut through the maze with a simple direction: "Let's find the most effective way to help as many children as possible." That summarized her objectives and influenced our decision-making. We continued a strong partnership with the Romanian Angel Appeal over the next decade and this resulted in long-term improvements in the treatment and healthcare for children and HIV-positive children. It was an enthralling moment in time and had set the future direction of our work.

CHAPTER 11

They Shoot Children, Don't They?

Investigating the Killing of Street Children, 1991

Olivia introduced me to Aninha Capaldi, the Brazilian wife of Jim Capaldi, from the band Traffic, and together we considered how we could respond to the phenomenon of the world's street children. At the time, the term "street children" wasn't in general usage, but after hearing that three children a day were being killed on the streets of Rio de Janeiro, Aninha's hometown, we decided that Brazil was the place to start.

During a two-week visit in 1991, we met with street children, government officials, media, NGOs, as well as the promoter of "Rock in Rio", the biggest rock event in the world. Everyone knew the streets were dangerous and that many died in drug deals, inter-gang warfare, and criminal violence, but dark rumours persisted that death squads were executing children in a drive to "clean up the streets". Equally disturbing was the apparent inability of the authorities to investigate these child murders or to prosecute the killers.

I saw the violence myself at dusk one evening as I was standing on the balcony of Aninha's flat in Ipanema, about five stories high, and peered down to the street below. It was like a scene from a science-fiction movie. There were many people on the street but they stood still. Like me, everyone was riveted as a policeman with a baton chased a young child. The kid, about twelve years old, was running for his life. He ducked and weaved in-between the bystanders. The policeman made gains on his prey and twice caught up with him. He brought down the stick on the child's back. As it struck him the sound was like thunder, and it made me shudder as I stood on the balcony watching the drama unfold below. It was over in a flash as the policeman chasing the kid disappeared from view and things went back to normal, with people going about their business. But I can still remember that moment and can hear the sound of the baton coming down on the boy's back. It makes me wince each time it comes to my mind.

We were told that children had left or been driven from their homes because of the breakdown of traditional family units, while a huge surge from the country to the city was causing urban turmoil. The cities in Brazil – and around the world – have continued to explode. In 1950, there was just one megacity with a population of more than 10 million – New York. By 2013, there were twenty-seven megacities, and for the first time in our history, half the world's current population of 7 billion lives in towns and cities. And this is set to rise. The UN predicts that these megacities will house 70 per cent of the people on earth by 2050 – 6.4 billion people out of a total 9.2 billion.

This explosive growth would occur primarily in developing countries. *Time* magazine reported that six of the world's ten fastest-growing megacities are in South Asia, in countries least equipped to provide transportation, housing, water, and sewers. Asia and Africa, now more than two-thirds rural, would be half urban by 2025. The number of abandoned children is expected to double, with child exploitation on the increase. This would contribute further to the sense of injustice and inequality among the world's poor that has driven extremists to seek violent solutions to the problem. With more than half the world's peoples moving from the countryside to the cities, how they adjust to their new habitat will define the twenty-first century.

The campaign to stop killing street children

On the flight back from Brazil we drafted a letter of protest that said simply: "Stop Killing Street Children". Signed by the Harrisons and the Capaldis, the signatures captured a glittering array of personalities, including Paul McCartney, Ringo Starr, Emerson Fittipaldi, and Richard Branson.

I realized that this was a significant development but wasn't sure how to make the greatest impact with such support. Our objective was to maintain control over the story, so that the emphasis of street children was not lost, the celebrities who supported our campaign weren't compromised, and that Jubilee Campaign's role wasn't eroded.

While we were wondering how to secure the story within the strongholds of Fleet Street, two of Britain's top journalists were making plans to work on a new investigation. Chief foreign correspondent Daniel McGrory and photographer John Downing were award-winning journalists who had maintained the *Daily Express*'s reputation as a major news force. John had recently been awarded the OBE for his work and was told, as a reward, he could report any story he wanted. John chose the street children of Brazil.

When we made contact, their response was immediate: "That's just the issue we want to cover!"

With Danny and John at the helm, we achieved all our objectives.

The *Express* splashed the story across the front page, with a banner headline showing a child in the cross hairs of a gunsight, summing up the risk these children faced. The story ran for four days and the letter of appeal, championed by the Harrisons and the Capaldis, was used, with Jubilee Campaign featuring in every issue.

This was probably the first time that street children had received such prominent media coverage. We regularly raised the cause of street children at the UN, and this combined activity helped to put the issue on the international agenda.

Ali Kimber-Bates worked closely with me on the campaign and she suggested that we always use capitals when describing these children to give them both recognition and dignity. She was right. And from that moment we referred to them as "Street Children".

Charity or pressure group?

When our friends, such as Petru in Romania and Alexander in Russia, asked for practical help, existing charities offered minimal support, if any. We responded because of our relationship with both of them, but I was cautious about plunging ahead and setting up a charity. Jubilee Campaign's activity was "charitable" but we hadn't registered as a charity and still operated as a pressure group. I didn't think the world was waiting for yet another organization and turned to a few people for advice.

Peter Benenson, the founder of Amnesty International, was a family friend and mentor. On learning that we couldn't afford a family holiday, he arranged for us to take a break in a new property near Oxford – before he had even taken possession of the home he was to retire in. I found his vision and insight was matched by his humility. He had a remarkable ability to grasp the roots of an issue, and had a towering influence in shaping my thinking and the mission of Jubilee Campaign. In one memorable conversation, Peter told me, "Don't duplicate in a small way what another organization is doing in a big way. Don't become a small version of a bigger organization merely copying what they do. Make your time count. Use your money wisely. Keep your commitment dynamic and personal to a specific group. Try to work where others aren't involved. In that way if you stop, you will be missed."

Peter's words made perfect sense and I followed his advice as if it was a guiding star advancing through the unfathomable universe. We registered a charity (Jubilee Action) in 1992 but kept Jubilee Campaign as a pressure group. Jubilee Campaign led the way by shining a light on cases and issues of injustice, while Jubilee Action provided practical support. At the time, charities were restricted in their lobbying activity, but to me anyway it had always been clear: our mission was about justice, not charity.

Ninety-five per cent of the donations were directed through Jubilee Action, as this enabled us to gain from taxable benefits and the charity paid most of the bills. But the arrangement left Jubilee Campaign financially weak, and a friend warned that this put me in a vulnerable position. As an employee of the charity, I could be fired or removed if someone wanted to take over, even though I was named as the "founder" and accepted by everyone in our network as the leader. The first chairman of the charity was a northern businessman called Andrew Smith, and he established strong foundation structures for the organization. Though we clashed at times, he told me he'd always be loyal to me, and our relationship survived and strengthened.

Jubilee Campaign worked alongside Jubilee Action in an effective partnership, and remained in harmony under my direction for many years. While Ann made religious persecution the main focus of the organization in America, I decided that our mission would seek to help children at risk.

I believed that our campaign in Romania and Brazil had set the direction for the future of our work. It wasn't something that I'd drifted into. In fact, the seed of the idea had been planted in 1987 on a visit to South Africa.

Lessons learned in South Africa

Paul Simon's *Gracelands* album was a hit but it was controversial. He'd recorded it with South African musicians in the country, thereby breaking a cultural boycott intended to isolate the apartheid state even further.

I liked the music but I thought he was wrong to have broken the boycott. I preferred the strident message of the song "No. No. I ain't gonna play Sun City" by Dylan, Springsteen, Bono, and others – even Miles Davis. The message was simple and direct. Bang. No compromise. No.

I was in South Africa a few years after *Graceland*'s release and met briefly a few of the musicians who played on the album. Those close to them told me that the connection with Simon gave them a boost and they felt that it helped lift South African music onto the world stage.

Visiting the country gave me a better understanding of the situation and alerted me to the tensions of getting locked into a fixed opinion on issues. It taught me to try to look objectively at things and not simply assume the role of a professional objector with a fixed position of a campaign machine pointed against everything. I thought we should design our campaigns based on what would really help to make a difference. And it had to be shaped by people who were directly involved and not from the outside looking in.

This was an important lesson, but South Africa had more to reveal. After visiting townships like Soweto and Khayelitsha, the sense of despair among local people was overwhelming. I was only in South Africa briefly, and at times I felt like a tourist on a drive-through, yet even a cursory glance made it obvious that apartheid was an unjust system and that people had the right to determine their own destiny.

It was in Khayelitsha in 1987 that I had a moment that moved me so deeply I couldn't find words to speak of it and never have until now. It came from nowhere. Some friends and I were visiting people in the township, and as we were leaving, I noticed an outhouse. As we walked past it, I opened the door and looked inside. The room was empty but there were two young girls, aged about five, playing on a foam mattress. They didn't have any toys or books but they looked content to be there. I learned that their parents worked as domestics in Cape Town. They left for work before dawn and returned home late at night. They probably saw their children rarely. Work was all they had. The people we visited kept an eye on the children.

I instinctively thought of my own kids. At home. Adored. Protected. I was sure that the parents of these girls loved their children as I loved mine, and worked so they could provide for them.

The experience never left me. I was silent on the drive back from Khayelitsha. With Jessica just two, and Rachel a newborn, I was basking in the joys of fatherhood, and was drawn to the notion of doing something to help children. I didn't know how to start or what to do, but I held this idea close until the time was right.

Brazil, 1993

Fernando Meirelles' critically acclaimed film *City of God* has been hailed as a classic of world cinema and chosen by *Time* magazine as one of the "100 greatest films of all time". The film's violent portrayal of life inside a Brazilian *favela* (slum) isn't a Hollywood concoction. In 1993 we were given a graphic first-hand account of life on Rio's mean streets by Roberto dos Santos, the leader of our project in Rio.

It started on 21 July, a blistering hot Wednesday. Police broke up a fight among street children over a box of glue. One of the boys was grabbed, bundled into a police car, and beaten. The police car was pelted with stones. "You'll regret this. We're gonna get you," a policeman yelled out.

Two days later, at midnight, three unmarked cars pulled up near the Candelaria Cathedral, a popular hangout for the kids who slept on the streets nearby. Roberto told me:

Six gunmen stepped out of the cars and headed for the sleeping children. They circled the kids and then opened fire at point-blank range. It wasn't a killing: it was an assassination. The killers shot the children in the eyes and in the head. Seven children died, one survived but passed away later in hospital. Two boys were grabbed by the gunmen and taken back to

their cars. They were executed and their bodies dumped at the
Metropolitan Museum of Modern Art.

Wagner dos Santos was one of the street boys who slept near Candelaria. He was grabbed by an off-duty policeman and shoved into a car. Forced to lie down with two other kids, one of the policemen sat on him and said, "You are going to die." Wagner was shot twice and lost consciousness. Hours later, he awoke to find himself in a park with his two friends lying dead beside him.

The killings made news headlines around the world. The President of Brazil flew to Rio and launched an investigation into the massacre and eventually the policemen were arrested.

Wagner recovered and was the first to enter a witness protection programme after deciding to give evidence against the officers implicated in the killing. He was attacked a second time in 1994. Fearing for his safety we worked with other groups and helped to move Wagner to Europe until the trial started in April 1996. Wagner returned to face his attackers in court and Marcos Borges, aged twenty-nine, was found guilty of murder. This was the first trial of its kind, a small step towards the march for justice.

In Britain, the parliamentary group was active and the diplomatic missiles were flying. Roberto told us that our campaign had played a part in influencing public opinion in Brazil and mobilizing international concern. This was echoed later in a message from Downing Street to us which said, "It is thanks to you that the urgency and importance of street children has acquired recognition."

In 2000, we linked up with the *Daily Mirror* on another investigation into the killing of children and they gave prominent coverage to our report "The Silent War", researched and written by Matt Roper. Veteran musician Peter Kirtley read the *Mirror* and was outraged. He wrote and recorded "Little Children" with the critically acclaimed jazz musician Liane Carroll. Paul McCartney added vocals and a short narrative. Radio stations plugged it, and even Virgin's Megastore on London's Oxford Street put the catchy song on its playlist.

David Alton stepped inside Brazil's killing zone in 2004 to investigate whether the murders had stopped. It wasn't good news. He wrote, "The scale of the killing is almost unbelievable. It flourishes in a climate of fear, silence and official collusion. The streets literally run red with young Brazilian blood."

In the north-eastern city of Recife near the World Heritage sites, David discovered "*favelas* and slums that shamed all of us. In these shanty towns, assassins roam freely with impunity and for as little as £2, will kill a child or adolescent who has fallen foul of the gangsters and the drug barons. A central cause of crime is the easy availability of small arms." David was told, "It is easier for a child to get a gun than to get a bus pass."

One of the key factors that exacerbated the situation was the flourishing drug culture. David observed:

> *Brazil ranks only after the USA as the second biggest consumer of cocaine. About 25 per cent of Rio's 12 million people live in their 680 favelas where there are several no-go areas controlled by rival gangs such as Red Command and Third Command who organize and arm the children. Children as young as four have guns and are used as "little planes" – to use the jargon of the street – trafficking drugs and messages between sellers and buyers.*

He commented that the fate of children living in a district known as "Inferninha" (Little Hell) reads straight from Dante. It is a place where the living might envy the dead. Inferninha is the area of Recife where child prostitution is concentrated. Here, at least forty children are known to be working as prostitutes – with more than sixty at weekends.

He learned that some of the boys and girls are as young as ten years old, and some were sent there by their parents to supplement their income. When Lord Alton asked whether the police simply closed their eyes to this, he was told, "No, they go to the bars every Tuesday for their share of the takings."

Dom Helder Camara, the Archbishop of Recife and Olinda, who died in 1992, was renowned for his outspoken opposition to the violence of the authorities and was a champion of the dispossessed. Dom Helder famously said that when he provided relief for the poor they called him a saint, but when he identified the causes of Brazil's acute poverty he was branded a communist.

It's evident that Dom Helder's prophetic words ring out as true, and are as relevant today as they were decades ago.

The boy I never knew

On our first night in Brazil in 1991, Aninha took me to a small downtown arts cinema to see a documentary about the transitory – and dangerous – life of children on the streets of Rio. Some of the street kids featured in the film were in the cinema and their raucous cheers announced their arrival on screen.

Aninha had met the street boys the previous night and over the next few days we got to know them better. There was Anderson: warm, loveable, who carried his books carefully, determined to complete school. Then Luciano: boisterous, loud, who pinched and hugged me, grabbed my camera, and took several shots from precarious angles. And finally Juanito: tall, gangly, a loner, reserved, often remote – in retrospect, someone I never got close to.

It was evident that each of them had done time at the dark end of Rio's mean streets. They went regularly to the Sao Martinho Shelter, a Catholic charity in the city, and this brought some respite. The boys were tough and streetwise, yet vulnerable and tender, like young adults who had bypassed childhood. Almost everyone wanted the same thing: a home, someone to care for them, to finish school, get a job, and settle down.

Juanito wanted to be a cook and spent much of his time in the shelter's kitchen. But he had problems fitting in and might have had learning difficulties. When asked what his ambition was, he replied wistfully, "To get a girlfriend but I'm too ugly."

Juanito was one of the boys selected to perform a traditional Brazilian dance for John Major, the only head of state to visit a children's shelter, Sao Martinho during the Earth Summit in Rio in 1992. Sometime during the festivities, Juanito drew close, oblivious to protocol, and extended his hand. In a flash of spontaneity, Mr Major clasped the palm of the boy who lived on the streets.

That moment was to become a tragic television epitaph. Four months after the encounter, Juanito was dead. He was shot in the head and the chest near his sister's home in the Favela de Nova Iguacu. We were passed a copy of the police file which we copied and sent to the Prime Minister and the All Party Group on Street Children. Mr Major wrote back and said, "Juanito's death is tragic news, but I am glad that the Brazilian Foreign Minister has promised to look into the circumstances. Our Embassy in Brazil will follow the investigation closely." We kept the pressure on and eventually were told that Juanito might have inadvertently annoyed a local gangster in the slums. The suspected killer died soon after in mysterious circumstances and that's where the police investigation ended.

Mr Major never forgot Juanito and wrote about his encounter in the House of Commons magazine:

I met Juanito at a shelter for Street Children in Rio de Janeiro. He told me that he first took to the streets when he was eight years old to earn money for his family. By day, he would shine shoes and wash windscreens. By night, he and his friends would sleep in doorways and watch out for police patrols. Juanito was one of the lucky ones. He had been helped by the team at the Sao Martinho Shelter funded by Jubilee which offers children a more stable environment and helps many find a better life. When I visited Sao Martinho, during the Earth Summit in 1992, Juanito welcomed me with a dance. I gave him an Aston Villa shirt. Four months later, Juanito was killed, shot twice. It was

a Sunday morning and he had gone out to buy some ice. He was
not more than seventeen years old. Juanito's murder seemed
to be without motive. He was not thought to be mixed up with
gangs or drugs. He was just a random victim of the senseless
violence which children face on the streets of Brazil and other
countries around the world.

I have often reflected on Mr Major's visit and what must have been
Juanito's proudest moment. For once in his life, he reached out
and someone was there to take his hand.

Mr Major was mobbed by the street kids at Sao Martinho and
genuinely moved by the experience. Aninha was on hand and
served as his interpreter, and when he asked her if there was
something more that he could do, she was ready.

She told the Prime Minister that girls on the street faced
harrowing ordeals as they struggled to survive. Some lost
their childhood, others their lives. Thrust into a vicious adult
world, girls as young as eleven and twelve had turned up at Sao
Martinho in desperate circumstances. Some were pregnant with
nowhere to go; others were on the run, after falling into petty
crime. Tragically, they were turned away as Sao Martinho had
no facilities for them, and neither did anyone else. There was no
shelter in the city that cared specially for girls.

"I'll see what I can do," he told Aninha.

True to his word, Mr Major made finances available for a
house to be bought for street girls and it provided shelter for about
twenty girls. The Girls Home became our first project in Brazil,
and Aninha worked hard with us to raise funds to keep it going.
For Rio's street girls, it was a dream come true.

Princess Diana wrote and told us of her interest in the home.
Her personal letter to me in 1992 expressed her feelings clearly:

I certainly do share your concern for the plight of street children.
I was very glad to hear of the practical ways in which you are

helping to improve their lives. I send my best wishes for your continued success.

We'd had word through her close friend Lucia Flecha de Lima, the wife of the Brazilian ambassador, that she would get more involved but it was not to be. Following her tragic death, we named the project "The Princess Diana Home for Street Girls" in her memory.

When Cherie Blair visited Brazil in 2001, Aninha showed her the impact made by the Girls Home. Aninha was impressed with her knowledge of Brazilian Street Children and the passion she felt for the issue, and one year later the Prime Minister's wife honoured us with a reception at Downing Street. It was a memorable occasion.

* * *

Many years have passed. Things have changed. I don't know if we ever got over the news of the falling of Juanito. In a way, Jubilee's mission to protect and care for children at risk unfolded more fully after our visit to Brazil. Aninha Capaldi and I have reflected on that first night at the cinema in Rio when she introduced me to Anderson, Luciano, and Juanito.

After the film, I bought chocolates for everyone as we stood in the cinema's lobby. Luciano immediately snapped his bar in half and handed half to me. I was reluctant to accept it but he forced the chocolate on me in a move that was both instinctive and affectionate. We shared a moment in time, exchanging gifts and each grateful to the other for the experience. But the gifts were different. Mine was superficial, purchased easily with a few coins, and could be replicated with ease.

The character of life is defined by such moments and the poignancy of the encounter has never left me.

CHAPTER 12

Human Wrongs

*Dying Rooms, Killing Fields, and Poison Gas,
1991– 2012*

With David Alton's strategic involvement, Jubilee Campaign developed an unrivalled parliamentary network in Westminster, while Ann Buwalda gained strong political support in Washington. Each year we returned to the United Nations Human Rights Commission to raise cases and issues of concern. Our organic growth eased our transition into an efficient, professional organization; I recognized the importance of business structures but had little interest in administration so left this to others.

I led the campaigns and instinctively knew what to do. Sometimes we had several campaigns running simultaneously, and it wasn't unusual to take phone calls from around the world or to meet with people from different countries all in a single day. Trying to recall such interlocking activity for this book has been challenging. Most campaigns evolved from a personal relationship: someone knew someone who had a problem and they would contact us to ask if we could help.

Hideout on Pirate Island: Hong Kong, 1997
Ten years after David Alton launched Jubilee Campaign in Parliament, we were making plans to publicize the landmark when the phone rang.

"A young Christian family have escaped from China and are hiding in Hong Kong. We need to get them out. Is there anything you can do?"

The newspaper headlines summarized the context. For the first time ever, Britain was to hand over a colony, once known as Pirate Island, to a communist state at midnight on 30 June 1997. Seven thousand journalists flooded into Hong Kong as the electronic media turned this extraordinary moment in history into a unique global event.

As I investigated the story, I was alarmed by contradictory reports from the diplomats and disturbed by reports that new laws meant that dissidents without identification papers (like the couple) would be arrested. I sensed the urgency with every passing hour. If we were going to help them, we had just twenty-one days left before the handover to communist China. It didn't take long to decide what I should do.

Armed with an appeal from David Alton to his friend, Chris Patten, the Governor of Hong Kong, I set off on the twelve-hour flight, relieved that an hour before my departure, confirmation had come through that I had a bed in the city, which was even more crammed with tourists than usual for the big event.

The story in Hong Kong was inspiring but alarming. Bob and Heidi Fu were leaders in the student movement in China in the late eighties and were among the radicals who protested in Tiananmen Square. Bob graduated in International Politics from the People's University and then taught English to the children of senior officials at the Communist Party School in Beijing. Heidi studied philosophy but also taught at a middle school in Shandong for two years. As prominent intellectuals, they were clearly destined for influential positions, but in the aftermath of the Tiananmen Square massacre, disillusioned with the system, they came to personal faith and joined a group of believers meeting secretly. Later they set up a training centre and became leaders in the underground church.

Problems emerged in 1996 when their teaching programme was exposed. Retribution was swift. They were arrested and jailed for two months. Following their release, Bob was dismissed from his job, Heidi was told that she would not graduate, and they were given two months to vacate their apartment. Surveillance increased as local police pressured them to reveal their contacts. A sympathetic insider warned them that they would be arrested shortly.

Convinced that they should leave, Bob and Heidi escaped from China – a story in itself – and went into hiding in Hong Kong. Assuming that they would leave for the West within days, they packed their suitcases and sat in a room, waiting. But days turned to weeks, and eventually, months. Almost a year passed. Their case had become unnecessarily complicated, with bureaucratic squabbles that left their situation gridlocked.

In April 1997, Daniel was born to Heidi and Bob in the Prince of Wales Hospital in Hong Kong. What should have been the happiest time of their life turned into a nightmare, but they remained calm. "We rely on God alone," Bob told me when I visited their flat, two hours after I arrived in Hong Kong, on a rainy afternoon in June. "We felt God was guiding us to take the dramatic step of escaping from China. We're in his hands."

David Alton's letter to the Governor of Hong Kong, Chris Patten, prised open the diplomatic world's inner chambers as I started to unravel the complications. The first hurdle was disinformation. The Fus had no chance of getting into a "Nordic country", as the US State Department had insisted. Sweden had already refused them. It was unsettling to hear some diplomats think that their case could still be worked on after the handover. I was determined that the politicians find another guinea pig for this bizarre experiment. The diplomats weren't prepared to be questioned and didn't respond positively to my challenges, but there was little they could do. As a result of David Alton's letter to him, Chris Patten had welcomed me.

The flurry of meetings, faxes, and telephone calls escalated over the next few days as I averaged three hours' sleep a night, desperately trying to find help. Someone. Anyone. Washington. London. Copenhagen. Paris. Even Tokyo. My phone bill resembled a telephone number.

In Washington, Ann Buwalda lobbied congressional offices and initiated direct legal intervention. On Monday, the US State Department's position was "We know one thing – they're not coming here." By Friday, the same official stated, "We know one thing – they are coming here."

The campaigning had worked and it ended just as it had begun – with a telephone call.

"It's the breakthrough we've been praying for!" Bob exclaimed. He could hardly contain his excitement.

Forty-eight hours before the deadline, their visa was approved and they rushed to Kai Tak Airport to start a thirty-hour journey, with two stopovers, that ended in North Carolina. Bob's message on our answerphone said it all: "We made it out of Hong Kong. Your visit was a turning point in our case. Thank you!"

I returned from Hong Kong, exhausted but invigorated. Working on Bob and Heidi's case had inspired me in a fresh way and convinced me that I had made the right decision by not staying in the office but leaving immediately for the danger zone of the diplomats' terrain. It was also a reminder of just why I had started Jubilee Campaign in the first place.

The dying rooms of China

In 2012, former BBC Chairman and Executive Chairman of ITV, Lord Michael Grade, chose True Vision's *The Dying Rooms* as his greatest documentary of all time. He told the *Mail on Sunday*, "I can't imagine how difficult it was for the filmmakers to get into China and to film secretly. You've got to take your hats off to them."

This was encouraging. I knew the team from True Vision and respected and admired their films. I considered them to be Britain's leading human rights investigative documentary filmmakers because they had consistently made outstanding films on social issues.

It started in 1995 when, as independent filmmakers, Brian Woods and Kate Blewett decided to investigate newspaper reports that baby girls were being abandoned in China and sometimes left to die in state orphanages. They travelled covertly and visited over a dozen orphanages in five provinces. Nothing prepared them for the discovery they would make.

Brian said, "There were times when we just broke down in the hotel afterwards. We were seeing some terrible things."

They filmed baby girls in dirty, soiled clothes tied to wicker chairs, their legs splayed. Underneath were potties and old washing bowls. Without toys or distractions, they rocked back and forward all day. Some children had learned not to cry out, because they knew that no one would come to their aid.

David Alton arranged for me to meet the filmmakers, and in a room in the Norman Shaw building in Westminster they laid out photographs from the film on a wooden table in front of us. I had to force myself to look at the pictures.

Brian explained, "The most shocking orphanage we visited lay, ironically, just twenty minutes from one of the five-star international hotels that heralded China's emergence from economic isolation."

Kate recalled the visit:

A disabled girl took me by the hand and pulled me into a darkened room. She led me to a pile of crumpled bedclothes and drew back the covers. A baby girl about eighteen months old lay there, fighting for breath, her eyes covered in mucous, her lips parched, her skin stretched tautly over her emaciated skeleton. She clearly had only hours or a few days to live. The staff told us that the girl had fallen ill, but as they had no medicines, they had simply put her in this room and closed the door. That was ten days ago. For ten days, she had lain alone in the dark, starving to death.

"We asked her name and were told Mei Ming. This means 'No Name'," Brian said. "Four days after we took her picture, Mei Ming lost her fight for life. She died of neglect. Her parents had abandoned her, and when we telephoned the orphanage, they denied she had ever existed. The only memory of her now is our film."

Titled simply, *The Dying Rooms*, Brian and Kate's harrowing documentary made devastating television viewing but also demonstrated how television could move people to respond.

Dr Stephen Mosher was the first American social scientist student to enter China after President Carter normalized relations with that country in 1979. He spent a year in South China, and lived in a country village studying family life. During this period, he witnessed how women who were six or even nine months pregnant were rounded up if they refused abortions. Their pregnancies were terminated in bloody conditions and some women were compulsorily sterilized. Dr Mosher's reports provided first-hand evidence of the abuse of women and first alerted the world to the vicious nature of China's population control policy.

China is the world's largest nation with a full 20 per cent of the population – 1.34 billion people. About one in every five people on the planet lives in China, but only 10 to 15 per cent of the land is suitable for cultivation. Concerned about the rapid growth rate, in 1971 the Chinese government aggressively promoted family planning and eight years later launched the controversial "one child policy". This introduced rewards and penalties to induce couples to limit their family to one child.

For years, Chinese cultural tradition dictated that every family must have a son or risk dishonouring their ancestors. Fireworks celebrated the birth of a boy, but girl babies were ignored. Abandoning children was illegal and carried stiff penalties, but parents seemed willing to take the risk because they didn't want to waste their only chance of a child on a girl.

Left by roadsides, riverbanks, and in railway stations, many abandoned children died of exposure, while others were picked up by gangs and used as beggars. State-run orphanages were under-funded and understaffed, and in some, the death rate for babies could be as high as one in five.

I felt privileged to be interviewed by Brian and Kate for their follow up, *Return to the Dying Rooms*, broadcast in January 1996. We were aware that it would create waves initially for groups within China, but it was an important issue and I was determined to stand with these dedicated filmmakers even though it meant I would probably never again get a visa to return to China.

The film featured Dr Zhang Shuyun, who had worked at the Shanghai Children's Welfare Institute, which had once been promoted by the Chinese government as a model of orphanages around the country. Dr Zhang had escaped with documents and photographs showing evidence of official indifference and brutality, and a report, *Death by Default*, was published by Human Rights Watch. She revealed that the majority of deaths that occurred from 1988 to 1993 were the deliberate result of "summary resolution". The purpose of the policy was to limit the number of children in order to maintain the workload at a constant level. When a new orphan or group of orphans arrived, childcare workers would agree among themselves to eliminate an equal number of the children already living on the ward, thereby holding the population constant. Once selected, the children would be denied virtually all food and medical care, and sometimes water. These children would simply become listless and fade away.

The Chinese authorities responded swiftly to Brian and Kate's documentary. The orphanages were traced and the directors summoned to Beijing. In an unprecedented move, the Chinese Embassy in London denounced the film as "a mean spirited deceitful fabrication". Their press release, entitled "The Dying Rooms turns out to be fake" asserted that the British film crew misrepresented a storeroom as a room where children had been left to die, and blamed Kate for the death of Mei Ming.

The Chinese said the film was "full of vicious fabrications and contemptible lies".

The Dying Rooms would eventually be seen by over 100 million people in sixty countries. No one could watch it and remain unmoved. It inspired people everywhere to get involved – by giving money, campaigning, or adopting an orphan. We worked with Brian and Kate, lobbying the authorities to improve the care of orphans, and the filmmakers set up the charity COCOA (Care of China's Orphaned and Abandoned) to provide direct support.

The film changed things. China slowly learned to trust the Western charities that have been working in its orphanages and now positively welcomes offers of help from some sources. In 2000, China changed its adoption laws to meet the needs of its orphaned children. Married couples with a child of their own are now able to adopt, as are childless couples. The adoption age was lowered to thirty, and fostering schemes were introduced so that orphaned children can be cared for in families rather than big institutions.

No one can answer the question of whether this is still happening today. Kate Blewett said, "The orphanages that we visited have been renovated and there are a lot of fostering programmes, so in some places there have been improvements but in others there have been none. China is a huge country and there are many state orphanages."

But there is hope. The COCOA team think that there is a will to change in China today, and they are determined to be at the forefront of those reforms.

The killing fields of Burma

As a child growing up in India after the Second World War, stories from Burma were all around me, as a close relative served as a doctor there. With the country about to fall to Japan, my aunt and uncle, Clive and Nora Egerton-Eyles, had decided they would end their lives if they were at risk of falling into enemy hands as prisoners of war. My uncle kept a revolver close at hand. They took the decision jointly after learning of the atrocities committed by the Japanese raiders and the Burmese soldiers who had joined them.

Under great duress, he placed his wife on one of the last evacuation planes out but couldn't be persuaded to join her. With a handful of medical officers left behind, these courageous doctors hung on until the final moments, and were among the last to leave as Burma fell. They literally walked out, trekked through the jungle, negotiated the mighty Irrawaddy River, and arrived in the safety of India, ragged and barely alive.

Their escape created a storm and my uncle was awarded an MBE, but it was not held in great esteem and he wanted to return it. The medal's resting place is now in a faded black leather case in a drawer in our home. The engraved insignia reads, "For God and Empire". It was his desire that more would be done for the Karen people – Britain's loyal allies – and he expressed shame for the catastrophic political fix that was to spell disaster for the country.

I was too young to grasp the issues and was easily distracted by the latest Beano or Roy Rogers comic, but later in life, I came to understand the rage he must have felt. I never imagined that one day I would be able to revive his dream or that I could play a part in offering some help to the people he could never forget.

* * *

For over sixty years, the Karen Army resisted the Burmese military's campaign of genocide against the Karen people, and this epic struggle has been called the longest-running civil war in history. The origins of the conflict are a gripping blend of murder, political intrigue, betrayals, and murky backroom deals.

Britain conquered Burma in the late nineteenth century and ruled the colony from India. Burma was strategically located along the trade routes from India to China, and, like India, was considered a jewel in the crown. At the time, the Karen were one of about 135 different ethnic groups including the Chin, Shan, Mon, and Karenni. The Karen homeland was an independent territory, rich in natural resources, and they were the majority there, with their own culture, religion, language, and institutions.

When the Japanese invaded in 1942, the Burma Independence Army, led by General Aung San (the father of the modern-day heroine Aung San Suu Kyi), joined the Japanese advance, fighting against British forces, wanting to liberate Burma from British occupation.

The soldiers loyal to Britain were the hill tribes – above all, the Karen. Britain promised an independent homeland to the ethnic minorities but after the war gave in to Burmese demands, and negotiated a deal with their old enemy, Aung San.

The Karen and other ethnic groups were excluded from the talks and their complaints that Aung San could not represent them were ignored. Stunned at the duplicity, the Karen, supported by Winston Churchill, watched with disappointment as Lord Mountbatten was used, by the Labour government, as an instrument in the negotiations.

The betrayal was complete in January 1947 when Prime Minister Attlee signed an agreement with Aung San for Burma to become an independent state; the new boundaries of territory included many ethnic minority regions without the consent of their people. This sealed the fate of the Karen, who viewed it as a double-cross by their "friends", and the Karen homelands were absorbed within a new emerging structure.

Six months after the agreement, Aung San and his cabinet were assassinated, and control shifted to Cambridge-educated Burmese lawyers, who declared independence in January 1948. They embarked on a violent purge in order to consolidate their newly gained territories.

The Karen felt their only option was to form a resistance movement to fight for independence. Predominantly Christian, the Karen reluctantly embarked on an armed conflict, convinced theirs was a just war.

Aung San's daughter, Aung San Suu Kyi and her party, the National League for Democracy, won a landslide victory in 1990 with 80 per cent of the parliamentary seats. The generals, now in power, placed her under arrest and cracked down on the party, while they continued to loot the country's natural resources and maintain a brutal campaign of genocide against the ethnic minorities.

In 1991 we hosted the Burmese government-in-exile for meetings in the House of Commons, and in 1998, David Alton undertook a clandestine mission into Burma. He observed, "The military have transformed the once peaceful land of Burma into a vast concentration camp, where genocide and ethnic cleansing occurs on a daily basis."

David was relentless in bringing this neglected issue to the world's attention. In one article, he wrote:

Britain promised the Karen an independent state but nothing was done. General Saw Bo Mya served in the Karen National Liberation Army, since his demob from Britain's Force 136 which bravely and valiantly resisted the Japanese during World War II. The General told me he blamed the British for the Karen's plight. He told me, "We are the allies you have abandoned and forgotten."

Inside Burma's jungles, a catastrophe is waiting to happen in a country with ethnic cleansing every bit as ruthless as Bosnia and genocide every bit as cruel as Rwanda. Atrocities in Bosnia shocked European sensibilities only because courageous reporters ensured that the story was told. Politicians reacted with international and judicial sanctions while trials for war crimes have been established in The Hague.

Compare that with our reaction to Burma. What is intolerable in Europe should not be tolerated in South East Asia.

Is a life in South East Asia worth less than a life in South East Europe?

With the media's focus almost entirely on democratic politics, we were determined to give voice to the hidden, less glamorous (and clearly more complex) issue of the ethnic minorities.

It was evident that the generals could only hold on to power because of foreign investments, but successful campaigning and shareholder pressure saw several famous names pull out – including PepsiCo., Texaco, British Home Stores, Heineken, Apple Computers, Philips, and Hewlett Packard. Levi Strauss put it this way: "It is not possible to do business (with Burma) without directly supporting the military government and its pervasive violations of human rights."

Not everyone agreed. Britain's Premier Oil, Suzuki, along with Total, the fourth largest oil company in the world, clung on. In a generation before Wikileaks, a damning piece of evidence revealed that the oil companies chose to ignore knowledge of human rights abuses, and that the Burmese military were paid to provide security on Total's projects inside Burma. One document known as "the Robinson cable" records a discussion at the US Embassy in which an oil executive, Joel Robinson, admitted that they (Unocal and Total) had knowledge of these charges. Aung San Suu Kyi distinguished the French oil giant by naming Total as "the principal supporter of the military regime".

Historians have reminded us that the Second World War was prolonged because of support for the Nazis. The US government's Eizenstat Report, in 1988, is explicit: 'It was a generally held view among Allied economic warfare experts early in the war that the German war effort depended on iron ore from Sweden and oil from the Soviet Union and that without these materials, the war would come to an end."

In a front page article in *The Guardian* (in July 2000), Premier Oil's chief executive, Charles Jamieson, insisted that any human rights violations they observed were reported to the authorities. Commendable, maybe. Maybe not. It was left to our parliamentary officer, Wilfred Wong, in the same article, to point out that the authorities to whom Premier Oil reported the abuses were themselves the abusers.

We joined other groups in challenging Premier Oil to get out (they did, in 2002) and encouraged drivers to target Total garages. With 1,444 petrol stations across Britain (and 12,840 stations worldwide), petrol and diesel vehicle drivers were able to send Total a distinct message. The power of choice. Thousands ordered our postcard with the stark message aimed at Total's chairman in prestigious Cavendish Square: "Making a killing in Burma".

We continued to lobby at the United Nations, but were dismayed at their policy of sitting-on-their-hands. The UN recognized that the Burmese military was an illegal government and urged an end to "systematic violations of human rights". But the UN would then extend its mandate for another year. During that year, the UN intended to investigate what it already knew. With a conference hall full of documents, the UN would simply update its catalogue of horrors, while the genocide continued. Who should be held responsible for this misery: the Burmese regime or the UN itself?

We helped a Karen pastor to set up a fish farm to feed a local community, but in April 2000 the Burmese military attacked the village and everything was destroyed. I explored the possibility of suing the Burmese military for the loss of our "enterprise" but nothing came of it. Despite this, we continued to send food and supplies through trusted contacts who risked their lives to take practical help to displaced Karen families hiding in the jungle, and in 2004 we started a goat farm at the Thai–Burma border. This simple but innovative idea was our attempt to directly help some of the neediest families with milk, as well as growing corn, soya beans, potatoes, and other vegetables.

* * *

We were not the only ones involved. I took a telephone call from a young man who said, "David Alton advised me to contact you. I've got this idea..."

On the last day in August 1999, James Mawdsley, then aged twenty-seven, slipped into Burma legally and calmly started to distribute leaflets. He was promptly arrested, and later sentenced to seventeen years in jail. I marvelled at his audacity since he'd already been arrested and deported twice but was shocked at the sentence. We had no option but to help and Jubilee Campaign led the battle for his release, working alongside his family. Our petitions and protests captured national media coverage.

One of our supporters paid for us to hire a ship for an afternoon and we packed it with James's family, friends, and supporters and sailed down the Thames. A TV news crew were on board and quizzed my daughter Jessica about why she'd joined the campaign for James. She rehearsed her answers with me. "It's just wrong, isn't it?" she asserted.

Halfway down the Thames near Tower Bridge, I felt a grip on my arm. It was David Alton. "Look at that. I can't believe it," he exclaimed, a tremor in his voice. I was stunned. A barge docked near the side had a banner that read "Landslides No Problem".

Some months earlier, an idea had come to David: landslides happen when small stones start to move. David had made this adage the focus of many talks, using the analogy of each of us being small stones; when we moved, great things could happen. I thought the idea was so strong that we wrote to all of our supporters in 1999, sending each of them a small stone in a mini-envelope. We asked them to keep it with them as a symbol of all those who were hurting, imprisoned, or separated from family and friends. David carried a stone with him.

We welcomed James's zeal and enthusiasm and were relieved (along with his family) when he decided, following his release in

October 2000, that his future activism would be conducted from outside the country.

There were many 'small stones' and many moments. Ben Rogers documented the situation in an important book on Than Shwe, the military leader who rose from a lowly postal clerk to become a brutal dictator. A young filmmaker left his career as a theatre director after an encounter in a refugee camp at the Thai–Burma border. Peter Summers, joined by his wife Emma, produced a film based on a promise they made to tell the story of these forgotten people. It was a moment that they could never forget.

Peter said, "That's the problem with those types of moments. They often break you, they always change you, they forever haunt you, but they never really release you."

I carry Peter's words with me. They expressed better than I could, just how I felt about our mission and my experience on this journey.

Today there are huge changes in Burma. Some speak of an "Asian spring". But what of the past? After initiating the first parliamentary debates (both in the House of Commons and the House of Lords) on the genocide against the ethnic minorities, Lord Alton declared, "One day I hope this evidence (the catalogue of human rights violations) will be placed before an international court, and as at Nuremberg, the perpetrators will be brought to justice."

Blind vision

David Alton put it this way: "A man with no eyes sees more clearly than we who have vision." He was describing the extraordinary blind Chinese activist, Chen Guangcheng, honoured by *Time* magazine in 2006 as one of the world's 100 most influential people speaking out for women "subjected to maltreatment that Beijing's own laws prohibit".

The familiar proverb that it is better to light a candle than to curse the darkness could have been written specifically for Chen

Guangcheng. Blinded by a fever as a boy, he studied law by asking friends to recite legal books to him. Guangcheng became the voice of China's powerless in 2005 when he challenged forced abortions and sterilization, defending disenfranchised peasants and the disabled. He said, "Someone has to fight for the people with no voice. I guess that person is me."

Mr Chen simply wanted China's leadership to enforce the laws it already has. But he was considered a troublemaker, and after a sham trail in August 2006, he was sentenced to four years in jail.

The charges against him were distinguished by their absurdity. He was found guilty of "damaging public property" and "assembling a crowd for the purpose of disrupting traffic" – even though he was under house arrest at the time. *Time* magazine reported that Guangcheng was accused of stealing water from fellow Shandong villagers by digging a well. During the trial, his lawyers were denied access to witnesses and materials, blocked from appearing in court, and beaten when they tried to visit Mr Chen's wife. Unknown assailants beat three other lawyers defending villagers jailed for supporting Mr Chen. David Alton met one of the lawyers, who told him he had been left for dead.

Guangchen thought the instigator of the attacks was a local official, Li Qun, who was party secretary of Linyi (in 2002–07), but no action had been taken against him. Instead he was promoted, and became one of Shandong's most powerful officials.

Our supporters distributed thousands of postcards directed at the Chinese authorities with the simple message "Free Chen!" David led our campaign, gathered support in Parliament, and raised his case with the Chinese authorities in London and China. In a 2012 article for the *Universe*, he wrote:

> *I campaigned for Mr Chen ever since he was arrested in 2005. Two years ago, while Mr Chen was still in prison, I met with Mr Chen's lawyers in Beijing and spoke to his wife by telephone. In 2009 at the Chinese Ministry of Foreign Affairs in Beijing, I*

met with China's Special Representative on Human Rights, Dr Shen Yongxiang, and among issues I raised was the case of Chen Guangcheng. I told him one day Mr Chen will be regarded as a national hero.

Guangcheng was released in 2010 but thugs and threats followed him like a shadow. His isolated stone farmhouse on the rural plains of Shandong province was surrounded by plain-clothes police and thugs, apparently hired at 100 yuan a day by the local government; over sixty security officials were involved in the operation. The windows were covered with metal shutters and the perimeter cordoned off with an electric fence. Floodlights illuminated the house by night. Authorities put seven surveillance cameras at the entrance to the village and around the house and installed cell phone-jamming equipment to prevent Mr Chen from having contact with outsiders. Visitors were refused permission to visit and even Hollywood star Christian Bale and a television crew from CNN were roughed up when they came calling in December 2011.

That changed when a video was smuggled out of his home and watched by millions on YouTube. Referring to his transfer from the Shandong jail to his home he said, "I was in a small prison and now I am in a larger prison." At the end of the YouTube video Guangchen said, "We, the sons and daughters of our great nation, should have the courage to defeat our own fear."

If the authorities thought things were under control, Guangchen's great escape electrified the world. Friends say that his escape was so well planned that it took local officials several days to realize that he was gone. He had stayed in bed continuously before escaping, and the ruse worked. His guards were convinced he was too weak to get away.

About 11 p.m., on 22 April 2012, as his captors slept, Guangchen scaled the compound wall. The next few hours were tense. He crawled through fields, hurt his foot during several falls, trawled through rivers, and evaded guards. Darkness was his secret weapon, a friend joked. Later, the celebrated artist Ai Weiwei tweeted, "You know, he's blind so the night to him is nothing."

Recalling the escape, Guangchen told a journalist on the phone, "It was extremely painful. I couldn't stand or walk. So I crawled." He struggled along stony ground, sometimes losing track of time. If he heard or sensed someone nearby, he froze in place, moving only when he thought no one would hear him. "I waited until the wind was blowing, or until the guards were listening to music on their mobile phones. Then I would start crawling again."

It took several hours to reach a prearranged point where He Peirong, a young teacher and human-rights advocate from Nanjing, also known as "Pearl", was waiting. Pearl drove him to Beijing, a journey that eventually led to the American Embassy and the bright glare of the international media spotlight. With incredible timing, he ambushed Hillary Clinton, who was forced to deal with the "crisis".

Over the years, the extraordinary journey of Chen Guangcheng has been an inspiration, a protest, and, at times, a dark farce. Now, through his own sheer will, his life came to symbolize an opportunity, for China and the United States. Guangchen was allowed to study in America along with his wife and two children, but I'm certain this isn't the final chapter.

Guangcheng's escape electrified Chinese bloggers who used the code-word from the 1994 film *The Shawshank Redemption* to circulate news: "Some birds aren't meant to be caged," they wrote. "Their feathers are just too bright."

No one was surprised when China's censors banned web searches for the word "Shawshank" on Weibo, the Chinese microblogging site (a hybrid of Twitter and Facebook), which has over 368 million registered users. "Chen" had already been banned.

Wanted Man

Joan and I encouraged our children to pursue their dreams and to study subjects they enjoyed – and so they did.

Luke's university degree was in computer games technology; for Rachel, it was childcare, and she worked with children, but her passion was to raise her own family. Jessica's curiosity touched on many things; she took a GCSE in law when she was thirteen years old – by then she'd learned how much lawyers earn. But she turned to fashion, and set her sights on the London College of Fashion (LCF). We knew it would be tough. There were 200 applicants for every place.

In 2001 I took her to the LCF's complex on Oxford Street for the interview, but afterwards she was despondent. She told me that she'd eavesdropped on the previous applicant's interview to give her an edge on what she'd be expected to answer. But when it was her turn, the examiner's questions surprised her because they were completely different. This convinced her that she'd failed. When she told me that she'd been asked about her interests, her favourite designers, and whether she made her own clothes (she did) I was certain that her sense of style had set her aside from the others, and persuaded her that she was wrong. I was delighted to be proved right, and in time Jessica received an unqualified offer from LCF (and went on to complete her fashion degree at Manchester's Metropolitan University in 2006). After she started at LCF, a lecturer told her that they could usually tell in the first thirty seconds whether a student would be accepted.

Jessica wanted to get her hair braided before she started college and had set up an appointment with a hair stylist in London. We were running late and grabbed a taxi to Notting Hill, and as we pulled up near the hair salon, the driver who'd been listening to the radio turned to us and said, "Did you hear that? A plane crashed into the World Trade Center in New York."

He turned up the radio and we sat in the cab for a few moments but the news was sketchy. We set off to a nearby shop, as Jess wanted some gum and a drink for the hours her hairstyle would require. We'd paid for the goods and were walking down Portobello Road, trying to locate the hair salon, when someone rushed into the street to alert passers-by that a second plane had crashed into a building in New York. Portobello Road seemed to come alive as people from shops shouted across the road to one another. A street seller called out to us, "It feels like the end of the world is on us."

For that instant flash it felt as though we'd become part of the secular prophecy that media pundit Marshall McLuhan had described as our "global village". Bad news had come from a far country; raiders had invaded. For a fleeting moment on the street we felt connected to each other with an impulse of common purpose. We had united against a shared yet unknown enemy.

We now know from the documentary *Manhunt*, which premiered at the Sundance Film Festival in 2013, that CIA analysts suspected al Qaeda and Osama bin Laden immediately. As the bin Laden legend swelled, revulsion mixed with intrigue about this jihad warrior who had forsaken great wealth to live frugally, inspiring fatal devotion from his followers.

Gwynne Roberts had been the first Western TV journalist to interview the world's most wanted man, and the photograph of them together in late November 1996 had a chilling intensity. I took the opportunity to quiz him in 2003 over a large cappuccino.

Gwynne told me that it had taken him a year to track down bin Laden, but I was surprised to learn that the key person who'd arranged the meeting was based in London. His story had the ingredients of a riveting spy thriller.

The London contact accompanied Gwynne to the outskirts of Jalalabad in 1996 but then disappeared for several weeks. He arrived suddenly late at night. Gwynne explained:

It was curfew hour, with no cars allowed on the street except for Taliban patrols. I suddenly saw my contact emerge from the shadows outside my hotel. He told me bin Laden had agreed to meet but we had to leave immediately. It was pitch black outside and nothing stirred on the street. He wore a cloak over his head as we walked together along the dusty pavement.

There were several checks to make sure they weren't being followed. Headlamps flooded the pavement with light and a Toyota Landcruiser roared up behind them. Gwynne recalled, "The door was flung open and I was pulled inside."

Inside the vehicle there were five Arab mujahedin dressed in combat uniform all armed with submachine guns.

The London contact warned Gwynne, "The Americans will do anything to find Osama. We can take no chances. If you have anything with you that could lead them to him you will not return alive from your meeting."

Gwynne recalled, "I felt sick to the pit of my stomach. There was no going back."

They drove for two hours along a track towards the mountains east of Jalalabad, passing several Taliban checkpoints along the way. The Landcruiser stopped in the middle of nowhere. "Under the moon, my companions got out, knelt, and began to pray."

Thirty minutes later, they reached a small temporary base with Taliban tanks ranged around the perimeter of the encampment with some 50 armed Arab fighters standing guard.

"After a body search, I was led into a tent and came face to face with Osama bin Laden himself."

I wondered what bin Laden was like as a person. "He's got warm eyes and comes across as hospitable, almost shy," Gwynne told me. "He was soft-spoken, and unexpectedly uncharismatic. His fingers were long and delicate, his eyes clear and direct. He did not look like a man who could be responsible for mass murder. Yet his words betrayed a darker soul."

That first evening they spent about four hours together and shared a supper of cold chips and chicken. Gwynne knew he could have been killed at any point. He recalled:

At the time, I didn't feel threatened but I suspect I might feel differently now. He certainly didn't give me the impression of being a psychopath, but when you listen to his words, you're

*aware that he's extremely tough and uncompromising. He
expresses himself in the language of a prophet and the only
person I could compare him with is Ayatollah Khomeini. I
experienced Khomeini's followers at his private mosque in
northern Teheran. Their eyes burnt with fervour, and they
knocked me aside as they burst into the building to listen to
his sermon.*

Bin Laden believed that terror was a justifiable weapon and
America and Israel were the main enemies. "Terror can be a
good thing and it can be a bad thing," bin Laden told Gwynne.
"To frighten innocent people without justification is a bad thing
and should not occur. But to terrorize and frighten oppressors,
criminals, and thieves is a good thing... so the terrorism we take
on is a good thing."

When Gwynne's interview with bin Laden was broadcast, it
received one of the highest ratings of the season, and remains a
document of historical importance.

Poison gas

Gwynne made his reputation as an investigative filmmaker with
some remarkable documentaries. In 1988, he uncovered the first
forensic evidence proving poison gas had been used against the
Kurds of Halabja, alerting the world to this massacre. Saddam
Hussein had singled out the small town of Halabja for attack,
because the local Kurdish population had sided with Iran in the
eight-year war with Iraq that had begun in 1980.

On 16 March, a helicopter flew low over the town, just 11
kilometres from the Iranian border, but no one paid it much
attention. Besides, the townspeople had grown accustomed to
shootouts and gunfire.

But this was different. Over three days, starting at 6.20 p.m.,
wave after wave of bombers attacked the town of 80,000 people.
Soon after the conventional bombing, planes dropped a lethal

cocktail of poison gas, according to BBC veteran reporter John Simpson, "nerve agents like VX, Sarin and Tabun, and the terrible but more primitive mustard gas, that dates back to World War I".

There was a smell of garlic and sweet apples as gas clouds hung over the town and the surrounding hills, blotting out the sky. The chemicals soaked into people's clothes, skin, eyes, and lungs. Five thousand died within hours. Entire families died as they sought shelter in their own homes. Thousands who tried to flee the town were trapped, their escape route blocked by clouds of deadly gases that had contaminated everything in their path. Others flung themselves into a pond to wash off the chemicals but died within minutes. Gwynne's award-winning film, *The Winds of Death*, carried haunting images: women and children struck down in the streets; cars filled with bodies; a father who tried to shield his twins from the poisonous gas.

Halabja entered the history books as the largest chemical weapons attack ever launched against a civilian population in modern times. The poison gas attack brought some international condemnation, but at the time, Saddam Hussein was essential to the Middle Eastern foreign policy of the world's most powerful nation, America. Iraq had been given tacit support by the West in its war with Iran, a war in which one and a half million people died, since Iran was considered a greater threat to the United States. Time passed, and Halabja was quietly forgotten by the world.

Ten years later, in 1998, Gwynne Roberts was smuggled back into Halabja. This time he took Professor Christine Gosden, a leading British geneticist, with him. It was a dangerous mission and they were protected by armed guards during their trip. After examining hundreds of local people, they recorded evidence of long-term irreversible genetic damage and discovered that the devastating legacy of the chemical attack lived on in the survivors.

There were many cancers, most unusually aggressive, some extremely rare, and numbers had multiplied alarmingly among children. Miscarriages and infertility had increased significantly.

Professor Gosden examined a foetus in the hospital and found that the unborn child had injuries consistent with chemical weapons poisoning. She was told that no one had recently given birth to a normal baby. Leukaemia, Down's syndrome, lung disorders, and heart diseases had all doubled, trebled or quadrupled in the town, while deformities such as hare lips and cleft palates had increased among newborn babies.

Gwynne's 1998 television documentary, *Saddam's Secret Time Bomb*, exposed an apocalyptic landscape with desolate people. Courageous doctors in a barren hospital did what they could in pitiful conditions. Needles were recycled, disinfectants and basic anaesthetics non-existent. The local orphanage had no stove or cooking facilities and only one dismal room to shelter the children.

Gwynne's film showed that Saddam Hussein, by this time demonized by the West, had been supplied with chemical ingredients by the same Western countries that backed military strikes against him and Iraq. Rolf Ekeus was the former head of the United Nations inspectorate charged with destroying Iraq's weapons of mass destruction (WMD) and he agreed to talk to the filmmaker.

Gwynne told me:

> *I interviewed Rolf Ekeus, one of the chief weapons inspectors and asked him if an agreement had been made between the UN and Saddam's regime not to reveal the names of companies which had supplied the ingredients for WMD. He said, no it didn't exist – on camera. Unfortunately for him, I had a copy of the agreement in my pocket to which he was one of the signatories. Of course, faced with the evidence, he had to admit that it was true.*
>
> *He said the agreement was reached because the UN inspectors felt they had to protect their sources. But how can you conduct an investigation on this basis? The UN showed itself keen to protect the economic interests of member states at the expense of the human rights of the Iraqi people.*

Ekeus, who went on to become Sweden's ambassador to the United States, said governments would "never have forgiven us" if the UN weapons inspectors had disclosed the identities of supplier companies.

Many of the shells found at Halabja had Soviet markings but who supplied the chemicals to Saddam? The questions rumble on today. An article on the BBC website in December 2012 noted, "With regard to Western companies, there is data pointing to 85 German, 19 French, 18 British and 18 US suppliers." Not surprisingly, there hasn't been a rush for answers.

I assumed that there wasn't anything we could do at that time (1998), given the enormity of the problem, but Gwynne said that virtually no aid had reached Halabja and things were desperate. "Anything you can do, no matter how small, would be useful," Gwynne told me.

I rang Ron George, of the charity World in Need, who introduced me to an intrepid traveller, Ray Scantlebury, who had made about thirty trips into the country during Saddam's reign. "It's dangerous. Saddam has a bounty on the head of anyone going into Kurdish territory."

With help of World in Need, we delivered supplies and equipment to the hospital and a fresh water well was drilled at the School for Orphans (in 1998), bringing uncontaminated water to the centre for the first time. We helped to run a music summer camp (in 2005) for youth and a music workshop. This was supported by a Kurdish master musician and held in Rawanduz, Erbil, and Suleymaniyah. I liked what Ray had set up. The Kurds have a long history of persecution and are one of the largest ethnic groups without a country of their own. Our music project taught traditional music to Kurdish children so that they learned about the history, folktales, and legends of their people but also continued the oral traditions so that this could be passed on to future generations.

With the fall of Saddam, it was hoped that things would improve; however, local residents still complained of the lack of basic necessities. In December 2012, the BBC reported that a chemical weapons expert warned that traces of chemicals were still being found in the town twenty-five years after the massacre.

A recent visitor to Halabja told me that people didn't want to move from their homes. All around were remnants from the attack, though the fields were fertile and local shops sold the produce from soil that has never been thoroughly tested. Some stone houses were still in ruins, while the graveyards were marked by jagged rocks overrun by fields of wheat and barley.

The one obvious physical sign of the tragedy was a simple memorial on the main road, depicting two figures in stone, of a man in a last futile attempt to shield his grandson.

CHAPTER 13

Rescue the Children

Inside Mumbai's Brothels, 1996–present

In 1996 I had organized a trip to India, and days before I was due to leave, a friend suggested I met someone he knew in Mumbai who had started to help people in Mumbai's sex industry. I'd spent several months there as a youth with Operation Mobilization but didn't think the city had anything special to reveal. A "high-tech" metropolis with real estate that matched New York in price, several blue chip companies had moved their back-office operation to the city. But on the spur of the moment I rearranged flights and setup a one-night stopover.

I arrived in Mumbai on a sultry evening in February and was met by Reverend KK Devaraj. It was humid and muggy and I was glad I was only staying twenty-four hours. I didn't want to waste a moment so we drove directly from the airport to Mumbai's red light district. On the way, he told me his story.

Devaraj was from South India but worked as an oil executive in Lebanon where he became a Christian. The experience led him to give up his job, and he returned to India in the early nineties though he didn't have a clear plan of what to do. Over the next three years, he befriended a group of boys in the Kamathipura area. It was Mumbai's oldest and Asia's second largest red light district and it had been set up in the 1880s during the British Raj as a comfort zone for British troops.

The boys Devaraj met were on drugs and he helped them to kick the habit and rebuild their lives. As he got to know them, he learned that their sisters and mothers were prostitutes. He won the trust of people in the sex industry because they had seen the impact on some of the boys. This contact gave him unprecedented access to the girls and women from the brothels who cruised the backstreets and alleys of Kamathipura.

Devaraj held church services nearby and the prostitutes would wander into the meeting and for that hour, business in the red light district slowed down. For a few minutes, the girls could lose themselves in songs of praise and prayers of hope. Amid such humiliation and shame, the women responded to a message of deliverance. Some of the children in the area attended the services and wanted to get away but he had nowhere to take them.

* * *

By the time we reached Kamathipura, light was fading. I could tell we were close, as girls with heavy make-up in brightly coloured saris lined the street corners in a silent parade.

Kamathipura's Fourteenth Lane snaked its way about 100 yards down; a muddy road with narrow houses on the left, mud huts and makeshift shelters on the right. There were ramshackle wooden buildings, each a different colour. Hands and elbows leaned on window ledges. Faces peered down. The girls had painted faces and brightly coloured bangles that jingle-jangled. Their eyes winked enticingly, but seemed strangely dead.

Mumbai's population numbered over 20 million. There were no accurate statistics on the number of commercial sex workers (CSWs) and estimates ranged from 50,000 to 500,000. Deveraj speculated that about 3,000 girls lived on Fourteenth Lane.

The women in the area trusted him so I learned their stories. Sharlinka wasn't sure how old she was. She was enticed from Andhra Pradesh with the offer of a job but was sold to a brothel owner. She'd been held captive for about five years.

"I had to work hard," she told us. "The men were fat, old, and smelly. I was forced to do some disgusting things. I wasn't allowed out for three years."

Another young girl with sad eyes said, 'I'm from Calcutta. I don't have any relatives, only a mother, but I'm not sure where she is now. I drifted around and ended up in Mumbai. I was caught one night by several men. They told me they'd find work for me, I'd have a good life, but I was sold into slavery."

She had graceful features but a dejected expression. When asked her age she speculated, "I'm about fourteen or fifteen, maybe even sixteen, but I don't really know." This girl said she didn't want to go back to the brothel and looked worried. "I don't have anyone in this world who cares for me. No one knows whether I live or die."

As she listened to Devaraj's words of encouragement, her eyes widened in silent wonder. It's as though she'd heard about some extraordinary discovery or the plot of an intriguing film. She hung on Devaraj's every word. Tears formed in her eyes. She bit her fingernails.

There were several Nepali girls with pale olive skin, soft features, and long angular bodies. Girls were trafficked from Nepal by underworld gangs with police collusion. They were held in a slave market, and brothel owners visited the auction to buy the girls. From Mumbai, some of the girls – and boys – were dispatched to Goa, now India's most popular tourist resort.

The girls sold to the brothels worked to pay off their debt. Customers paid the brothel and the girls survived on tips. This system of debt bondage kept them in virtual slavery. They were held in appalling circumstances, beaten and abused, with little opportunity of ever being liberated from this vicious circle of servitude. In many cases, the girls had no idea when their debt would be paid off – if ever – and were resigned to a life of enslavement. They charged, so I was told, between 50 rupees (£1) and 250 rupees (£5) and yes, everything was available with no limits to these sexual encounters.

Mumbai's red light district had a heavy gang influence and there were many incidents of shootouts and stabbings.

Suicides were spoken of factually. Anyone caught trying to escape was beaten severely when they returned. One girl, Mina, tried to jump out of a top-floor window but fell and broke her back. She had been caged for seven years and was forbidden to leave her room. Usually the girls were confined for two to three years before they were allowed out on their own.

Night had fallen and the backstreets of Mumbai were packed with girls. A narrow space between the buildings revealed an alley, an active corridor leading deeper into the quicksand. A furtive glance into the warren exposed more verandas, more bright saris, more girls. Somewhere from the midst of the labyrinth, a baby cried, an old man sat crumpled, staring into the distance. Life went on.

Asha's story

Devaraj told me there was a girl he wanted me to meet and we tramped back and forth through the alleys and dark, narrow passageways trying to locate her. It was late at night but the streets were crowded and dirty. A woman scavenged through rubbish that was piled up at least 15 feet high, sprawled everywhere. A child ran across and kicked the garbage playfully. No one stared, no one was surprised.

After twenty minutes, we learned that the girl we were seeking was at a nearby school where floor space was provided for a few destitute children to sleep. "She's safe for a few more hours," Devaraj sighed. "I don't like her being in this area at night. It's just not safe. Anything can happen."

The school had locked its gates because of the lateness of the hour, but she was summoned, and after ten minutes an elegant, slender, and strikingly beautiful young girl appeared behind the bars of the gate. She talked for a while, while I stayed back in the shadows, observing the scene. In the dim hallway, a coloured light from a nearby neon sign shone on her.

It was hard to define, an inexplicable, timeless moment. I didn't know her name but felt stirred. Here amid the rubbish, squalor, corruption, oppression, and overwhelming desolation; here in this slave kingdom of girls with painted faces, she glowed like a precious jewel. I wanted to capture the spirit of this defining moment and the scene around us but it was too dangerous to sneak a photograph. As we retraced our steps and walked back to the car, I heard her story.

Asha's mother had been a prostitute who lived on Fourteenth Lane, just around the corner from the street of shame that we'd just walked down. She had grown up in a cramped, squalid room, virtually a cage, where her mother serviced between ten and twenty-five customers a day. Most of the time, Asha and her younger sister and brother were forced to loiter in the street, but many nights she fell asleep, curled up in a corner of the room, waiting for the last customer to leave.

When her mother died, there was no time for tears. The brothel owners moved a young Nepali girl into the cage, and Asha and her younger siblings were dumped in the street outside the brothel where her mother had worked. A makeshift canvas hut granted sanctuary from the scorching summer heat and the driving monsoon rain.

The young urchin family ate leftovers given to them by friendly prostitutes, scrounged scraps from the rubbish dump, and begged for *paisa* from passing trade. Their survival was a remarkable record of resilience amid grinding despair and degradation.

The brothel owners kept a custodial eye on Asha and her sister, as, inevitably, the children of prostitutes always followed their parents into the sex industry. The word on the street was that Asha's mother's boyfriend, a taxi driver, lied and said that he was her father, and was negotiating a deal with one of the brothel-owners, expecting about £600 for the sale of his beautiful young daughter. That was a small fortune, and money he just couldn't refuse.

The turning point in her life came when she met Devaraj and told him that she wanted to escape. His reply was, "Have faith. With God everything is possible." But with each passing day the tension was mounting. She was repulsed by the sexual remarks from local men but there was no escape, nowhere to hide. Every time she spotted the chubby church worker, she chased after him and tugged at his sleeve. "Uncle!" she'd call out. "When will you take me away?"

Asha wanted to turn her back on the past. She wanted to wave goodbye to Fourteenth Lane forever. She told him:

> *I want to leave. I feel dirty here. I'll never forget this street but all the memories are bad. I don't like the way the men look at me. Some men want me to go with them. They say they'll look after my brother and sister. I sense the danger. Every day it's getting harder for me to live here. I know I can't fight them forever. It's a question of time. I want to leave here but I have nowhere to go. No one wants me except the brothel owners.*

The next day, Devaraj had arranged for some of the girls, including Asha, to meet me at his office and I was struck at just how young and fragile the children seemed. They were dressed smartly with their hair done. One by one they lined up against the wall and I took a portrait photograph of each of them. Asha, the oldest of the children, was last. She faced the camera. Her eyes were alive with the half glint of a smile. The awkwardness of the meeting and the formal soundings seemed an obvious contradiction to their life in Kamathipura.

It was time to leave Mumbai, and as Devaraj drove me to the airport, I asked what would become of Asha.

"The daughters of prostitutes have all followed their mothers into the sex business," Devaraj said. "Very few get away alive."

"But could she be rescued?" It was the question that I carried with me.

Devaraj felt that the only way to make a difference was to establish a residential home outside the city where orphaned and abandoned children of prostitutes could find sanctuary. It seemed an insignificant gesture given the scale of the problem but if we couldn't rescue Asha, it's clear she would be condemned to a life sentence of sex slavery.

On the flight back home, the image of Asha alone in the red light district haunted me. With it came the realization that if we were unable to purchase a building, the doors of another house would open for Asha and her life would alter forever.

It was a race that I was determined to win.

A home for Asha

Backstage politics created tension within the office circle, as there seemed an unwillingness to support this new project. I took the materials home and over the weekend the family helped as we bundled hundreds of letters that I had personally signed with photographs from my trip, and posted them. I was concerned about the photograph of Asha. It didn't have the dramatic impact that such images needed to grab people's attention. Still, it seemed to have a power as many people were moved and responded generously.

This had become a personal mission and I treasured each response. As with other projects, 100 per cent of every donation went directly as designated and within a few months we hit our target. Devaraj had found land two hours outside Mumbai and personally designed a grand house that was built in record time. Finally, we had a home for Asha.

A few months after my visit, Asha collected all her belongings into a cardboard box and waited at the corner and, when the car pulled up to rescue her, she climbed in and never looked back at Kamathipura's Fourteenth Lane. Four other girls came with her, including her sister, and also her brother.

The money had come from many directions, mostly individuals

with small, sacrificial offerings. One of the larger gifts was given by George and Olivia Harrison, who both took a personal interest in Asha. Her story had touched them and they wanted to help.

George had a great love for India and he was moved by our mission to rescue children from sex slavery. He held one of the photographs of the girls at the home, studied it closely, and told me, "Make sure that you use reliable builders and that they use good-quality materials. These houses must be built well and be strong."

When the *Beatles Anthology* was released, George suggested that a portion of the profits should go to charity, and our work in India was one of many to benefit. With George and Olivia's donation, through the Apple Foundation, we were able to pay the entire running costs for the home for a year. After George's death, "My Sweet Lord" was re-released and hit number 1 in the charts with the profits going to good causes, and Olivia remembered us and donated a generous amount to this work in India. She said, "George was very interested in Jubilee's work in India, having spent so much time there and having such love for that country."

Steve Brown had kept in touch since the days he had helped us with our campaign for Romania's orphans. He was managing Billy Connolly and told me they had announced a benefit concert during Billy's five-week sell-out residency at Hammersmith's Apollo Theatre in 1997 and asked if we needed money. I sent him three projects to choose from. Steve told Billy about our plans to build a home for orphaned and abandoned children of prostitutes and showed him my photograph of Asha.

Billy walked on stage clutching her photo and for the first few minutes of the show he spoke movingly about Asha and explained where the money from that night's performance would be spent. He then delicately placed Asha's photograph on the wooden stool beside him, and then started his act. Within minutes he had his audience in stitches. While 3,000 people in the theatre were crying with laughter, almost falling out of their chairs, I sat riveted in my seat in the tenth row with tears of joy rolling down my face. I could see Asha's photograph in front of me. She seemed to be looking directly at me. She was smiling.

Billy's concert produced a phenomenal amount of cash. We had the choice of playing it safe and keeping the money for several years' running costs for the home, or we could build another home, so that even more children could be rescued.

Within a few months, a second, equally impressive home was built, again from Devaraj's original design, and over the next few years more than a hundred girls were rescued from Mumbai's red light district. Each one told an extraordinary story.

When I raised the difficulty of recurring operational costs for both homes with Steve Brown, he came up with the brilliant idea of launching Tickety-Boo Tea, with all the profits used for the project. A deal was arranged with Nadeem Ahmed for his company Global Tea and Commodities to source, produce, package, and distribute the tea.

In October 1999, Billy invited the media and friends for a day on a tea clipper that sailed down the Thames and launched the innovative idea. My daughter Jessica, aged fourteen, took a day off school (with my approval) and joined me on the best "day in the office" that I'd had. Billy was just brilliant and the coverage was fantastic. The clipper was packed and everyone wanted to hear him tell the story of why he launched Tickety-Boo Tea.

On the way home that night, Jessica and I stopped off at Tesco and we hugged each other when we spotted Tickety-Boo Tea on sale. Everyone who bought Tickety-Boo Tea contributed towards the running costs for the homes for several years. Even I became a tea drinker.

But the pressure was turned up when some big supermarket chains were unable to give shelf space for the "chari-tea" and we were again faced with the challenge of raising the operational costs.

Rachel's dream trip

My daughter Rachel had become a pen pal with one of the girls at the Jubilee Homes and regularly donated some of her pocket money to the work. She desperately wanted to travel to India to visit the girls but this was unlikely to happen. She was thirteen but also was extremely ill with chronic fatigue syndrome (ME) and only attended school for a few hours each week. Undeterred, she began saving money for the trip. We didn't discourage her because dreams and goals are useful when you have a long-term illness. As months turned into years, her travel fund grew, and though her illness continued, her stoic determination to live a full life in spite of sickness began to conquer the disease.

Maybe it was because she was immobilized for several years that she developed a passion for adrenaline sports and, much to our horror, discovered catapult bungee on one of our summer holidays. Interestingly, it had a positive effect on her illness as the adrenaline seemed to boost her metabolism. Meanwhile her loud and uninhibited enthusiasm for the catapult bungee attracted crowds, and the owner of the sports attraction gave her free jumps for drawing more people to the venue.

As she got older, the bungees got higher; when she learned that we wanted to start a new home for AIDS orphans, she decided to raise funds through a sky dive. I was inspired but nervous. Rachel's jump, in September 2004, raised a phenomenal £75,000 from generous Jubilee supporters that secured matched funding from the Laing Trust in the UK, and from a similar arrangement through Ann Buwalda in the US. As a result, we secured all the funds to build this new home and its operating costs for three years. On hearing this story, our Dutch partner, Dirk Jan Groot, paid for Rachel to fly out to India to visit the homes. She arrived just as the foundations for the AIDS Home were being laid. She achieved her dream. It was a powerful demonstration of the difference we can make with imagination and commitment.

Rachel spent a memorable week living with the girls at the homes and wrote this heartfelt poem on her return.

The Children Whom Life Forgot

In the bright sun these children play
The lucky few who got away
They were picked up, they were helped out
They were shown what life's all about
Here they are happy, here they run free
But they need no reminder of how their lives could have been
Before they were freed, their lives were a shock
These were the children, of whom life forgot

They once lived in hatred, in dirt and in fear
And if they cried for help, no one would hear
Their lives had no meaning, no future prepared
And in this vicious circle, no girl would be spared
For in any second, as time moves along
They'd be forced into the life, which had just killed their mum
Then in the blink of an eye, their childhood is gone
There's no time for growing, as life must go on
They'll soon become masters of the trade
And have children whose life will be just the same

Imagine a life with no hope and no meaning
Imagine a house with no walls and no ceiling
Imagine being taught to expect nothing from life
Imagine waking each day to more pain and strife
Imagine looking down the street, knowing that's all you've got
Imagine knowing you're the child of whom life forgot

These few lucky children whose lives have been spared
Now live for a reason, their future's been paved
They carry a spirit, which cannot be measured
They live a rich life, which doesn't need treasures

They've learned life's big secrets, its lessons we're told
They know the life they're living is richer than gold
They now have a purpose, their name means a lot
They're no longer the children of whom life forgot
For now, these bright children play under the sun
Their lives once forgotten have now just begun

* * *

In 1971 George Harrison had organized The Concert for Bangla Desh with an all-star cast that included Bob Dylan and Eric Clapton. It was the first ever rock charity event and set the template for Band Aid, Live Aid, and all that followed. When the DVD/CD was remastered and released in 2005, Olivia directed a generous portion of the profits to our work in India through the George Harrison Fund for UNICEF. The donations helped us through a critical time.

Many who heard about the rescue mission in Mumbai wanted to see the Jubilee Homes but there were sensitivities and we restricted visitors. We made an exception for Hamish Dodds, President of the Hard Rock Café, and he visited Mumbai in 2007 and heard the personal stories himself: the girls who were tricked and trafficked, the children saved, each with their own story of redemption. He told Devaraj, "I was truly impressed by the passion and dedication you and your teams have. It was very clear to me that the task you have ahead of you is immense but you really do have the opportunity to make a difference in so many people's lives." Hamish determined that they would not be forgotten, and Hard Rock Café became fervent supporters. We needed them.

* * *

It hasn't been easy for Asha. She was hospitalized for TB, struggled with her studies, found it hard to fit in with the others in the home, and experienced predictable teenage problems. Although cheerful and bright, she had a melancholy side, and one evening when I was in Mumbai, she told me, "I'm sad but I don't know why."

Overcoming tremendous obstacles, she enrolled at one of Mumbai's top colleges. But the students found out about her background and she had to endure their taunts. She was resilient and strong and faced her accusers head on – a challenge she eventually triumphed over.

In 2002 she married Sanjay, and Devaraj awarded me the honour of giving Asha away – one of the most special days of my life. The wedding was planned for 25 June but it was also the day that the newspapers predicted would be the heaviest rainfall of the monsoon season. Everyone prayed that the rains would be delayed by twenty-four hours, and with extraordinary timing, the cloudburst came just hours after the reception ended. We returned to our hotel, soaked but elated, fired with a sense of fulfilment and blessing.

Asha and Sanjay were employed by Jubilee Campaign, working with Devaraj's outreach programme in Mumbai, and she personally rescued children at risk. Devaraj was an inspiring figure and over time we developed a strong partnership with his organization, Bombay Teen Challenge.

Baby for sale

The local municipality in the red light area was impressed with Devaraj's work, and in 2000, they offered us premises to operate a shelter for the children of prostitutes. The shelter was ideally located in the centre of Mumbai's sex industry and would provide prostitutes' children with a safe haven at night, the moment of greatest risk. The children were looked after during the day and encouraged to attend school. The shelter gave us a foothold inside the sex trade and increased the team's influence. It enabled us to keep a watchful eye on these children as they grew and helped to prevent them from entering the sex business.

The property required refurbishment and we designated funds from George and Olivia Harrison towards these costs. I asked Devaraj how we could be sure it would be used for children at risk and not just poor children. The question was answered – like many others – with a telephone call.

"There's a baby for sale in one of the brothels. She's about to be sold," the man said. "Come quickly or it'll be too late."

Devaraj broke off his meeting in the office and drove directly to Kamathipura.

The nine-month-old girl's father worked as a street labourer, the poorest of the poor, in Mumbai's bustling vegetable market. Tragedy struck when the child's mother died. In turmoil, unable to cope, and with intense financial pressures, the father took his daughter to Kamathipura, the centre of the sex industry.

The man toured the brothels and, in a moment of madness, offered the baby for sale. The news caused a sensation as the brothel owners bargained over the innocent child. The man was offered £150.

The money was a significant amount for the labourer. Just as he was musing over the deal, Devaraj burst into the airless room located at the back of one of the brothels. After some discussion, Devaraj realized that the labourer was determined to sell the baby. Taking him aside, Devaraj warned that there would be consequences and convinced him not to sell the child. The father eventually handed the girl into our care.

Devaraj accepted the child immediately. Any hesitation would have been catastrophic and the child would have been sold. The rescue completed, the baby was safe. She was named Glory. She was taken directly to our shelter, the first child to be given refuge.

I was in Mumbai as this remarkable story unfolded. I held Glory in my arms shortly after her deliverance and thanked God for the miraculous timing that enabled Devaraj to rescue this special child. It was appropriate that this millennium baby should be given freedom and a new life as a symbol of the beginning of a new century.

CHAPTER 14

Kids Behind Bars

Law Changed to Get Children Out of Adult Jails, 2001–05

I was inspired by the filmmakers at True Vision – Brian Woods, Deborah Shipley, Jezza Newman, and Kate Blewett – because they didn't just produce good documentaries; they wanted their films to make a difference. I was privileged to be involved with them on films such as *The Dying Rooms* and others.

In 2001, the BBC broadcast their 98-minute investigation into children in prison around the world. The documentary, called *Kids Behind Bars*, took us on a journey into countries as diverse as India, USA, and Brazil. Their secret was to let the children tell their own story and to allow this to unfold without sensationalizing the material. It proved to be a winning strategy.

In Mongolia, we met Tsenguunjav. Officially his age was estimated at twelve years but he looked no more than eight or nine. Caught in the wrong place at the wrong time, with a stolen mobile phone, the lad was nailed for the theft, accused by the real thief. Tsenguunjav was in a tiny cell with twelve other boys. Several of the youths had been in the cells for months because the Mongolian legal system insisted that children must be accompanied by a parent when they appeared in court. Because Mongolia was one of the last actively nomadic societies in the world, the police had difficulty tracing parents. As a result, children languished in detention for months.

When Jezza Newman discovered Tsenguunjav he was trembling with terror. The young boy had no idea what would happen to him or when, if ever, he would see his family again. His cellmates had scared him further with made-up threats claiming that he'd be sentenced to several years in prison. Tsenguunjav was just one child among thousands, probably hundreds of thousands, who have been unjustly treated – a statistic lost amid the monolithic anonymous system that can't or won't spend the time to investigate individual claims of children who had no protector or guardian to resolve their case.

And that's probably how things would have stayed for Tsenguunjav. But he was destined for something else.

True Vision gained permission to film in Mongolia through the Royal Ulster Constabulary (RUC) who had committed to train the Mongolian police; as part of this exchange, RUC Chief Constable Sir Ronnie Flanagan was on a visit to Ulaanbaatar. Sir Ronnie had piloted the RUC through many years of "The Troubles", but when he learned of Tsenguunjav's case and met the youngster in jail, he was moved to tears. Sir Ronnie demanded that the boy be released, and Eastern hospitality meant his request was granted. Tsenguunjav was placed in a refurbished Save the Children home until his parents could be traced.

Kids Behind Bars is still the only global documentary on juveniles in prison and afforded a voice for children like Tsenguunjav to tell their own story. The torment was both in what was revealed and what would have been forgotten, but for their film. This was investigative reporting at its greatest.

The same year (2001) we had started a human rights magazine called *Just Right*, and I asked the filmmakers if we could use some of their material in it. They agreed and wrote a special feature explaining why they had made the film. We dedicated that entire issue of *Just Right* to the film, with original articles, interviews, and images from the documentary, and our magazine was offered to people who contacted the BBC after its broadcast.

Edwin's story

Kids Behind Bars made powerful television and I couldn't sleep that night after watching it. The faces of the kids kept coming to my mind, and on one of Father Shay's visits to the UK, we talked about this issue. "Kids are still in jail in the Philippines and detained with adult prisoners," he said. "It's a scandal."

He told me the story of a young boy called Edwin and later wrote an article about him for *Just Right*. It all started with a cheap, tacky necklace not even worth £2, explained Father Shay. The boy had snatched it from a market stall, but before he could run, he felt a firm grip on his arm. He'd been nabbed.

The owner of the stall was a vindictive, bad-tempered woman who insisted on reporting the slim fourteen-year-old youth, Edwin, to the local *tanods* (police aides), many of whom are bullies and lord it over the poor. The *tanods* and the uniformed police patrol the backstreets and slums and appear to uphold the law but many turn the other way, too busy protecting the drug pushers or collecting their daily payoffs from the local operators of illegal gambling dens.

The vendor insisted on pressing charges and Edwin was hauled to the local police station and roughly pushed inside, his arm twisted behind his back and a gun bashed against the back of his head, causing intense pain. For the police, his arrest meant more paperwork. They were annoyed and took it out on Edwin.

Edwin was thrown into a tiny cell packed with a dozen other street kids in ragged, dirty T-shirts and shorts, emaciated and starving. Their thirst was intense in the overpowering hell-like heat. Neither Edwin nor the other street kids were given any food in the police holding station, as that is considered the family's responsibility – if they have any relatives. The police didn't send for Edwin's parents, although this is a legal requirement; but it seems the law is for others to obey, not them.

Like Edwin, at that time thousands of kids were held illegally in prisons and holding cells all over the Philippines. They didn't have parents or anyone who would stand up for them and defend their rights. Most had been abandoned and lived for years on the streets, begging and loitering at the markets. They got food hour by hour. But there was no schooling, no home, no love, no friendship – nothing!

When the slim youth wasn't home by dark, Edwin's two older brothers went looking for him. It was 7 p.m. when they learned that he had been arrested and they hurried back to tell their parents.

Edwin's mother scrambled some food together and rushed to the jail. The family sat with him all night. Edwin squatted by the cell door, terrified of what was going to happen to him. If he was charged with theft of the necklace, the sentence could be five years' imprisonment as an adult criminal and he would be jailed with rapists and murderers – a cruel punishment for a mere fourteen-year-old youth. Shay put the case in perspective: "For that simple mistake in a moment of temptation a life was to be lost."

It seemed an extraordinary contradiction that at the start of the twenty-first century – a time of unparalleled technological breakthroughs and public awareness on social issues – children like Edwin could be jailed with adult prisoners. Holding children in cramped, overcrowded cells, detaining them with adults for indefinite periods of time, in torturous conditions, and providing no legal assistance, prison turned children into criminals instead of turning them from crime. A Juvenile Justice Bill, which would have put a stop to this in the Philippines, had been stalled in the political system for years.

Campaign launched

Shay and I decided to launch a campaign to get the law changed and we mapped out a strategy over a coffee at our home. We designed postcards calling for the Filipino authorities to pass legislation on the issue and scribbled out the text for a petition aimed at getting the UN involved. I wanted to publish a report and Shay agreed to help with the research. He said that we could include his organization's year-long investigation of children in jail. I contacted our friends at True Vision and told them of our intentions to build on their pioneering work and was pleased with their endorsement of our plans.

I wanted our report to include material from other countries; the information was scarce, and I asked our researcher on the project to track down UNICEF's leading expert on juvenile justice, Geert Cappelaere. It took two weeks and we finally reached him in May 2005 while he was on a visit to Africa. All he could say was, "It is impossible for me to give you an exact figure on the numbers of children in prison." We continued to press him, and one month later, Mr Cappelaere went on the record saying the following:

Very few countries make information available on the issue of kids behind bars. It isn't that the information is hard to find but that most authorities are not forthcoming. The most widely accepted estimate, which was made four years ago now, is that the number of children in prison is about 1 million.

There was a growing consensus among the team that this was becoming an important campaign as very little was known and even less was being done about the problem. We knew that we couldn't reach into every prison in the world and unlock the cell door so decided that our campaign would focus on the Philippines, where the information was comprehensive and authoritative. We'd already agreed with Shay that our target was to seek legislation to stop children being imprisoned in adult jails.

We always used photographs and graphics prominently in our campaigns and we knew immediately that the image for this campaign should be a photograph that Shay had taken years earlier of a six-year-old child called Rosie. She was behind bars, clutching a can of Coca-Cola and crying her eyes out for her mother. Shay had demanded that she be set free – and she was.

We used Rosie's image on all our campaign materials as a symbol of children imprisoned around the world.

While we continued to research the report and prepared the materials for the campaign, I started on our final objective – I wanted to get coverage from television and the print media to report the story.

It was a risky assignment because it meant going secretly into the jails and filming undercover with Father Shay's assistance so we needed journalists we could trust. I contacted Hazel Thompson, who worked for all the top international publications, but she was freelance and relied on regular work in order to supplement projects such as ours. I had worked freelance myself so understood the financial pressures she faced. She was enthusiastic and looked at dates when she could start.

Around the same time, I met with television journalist Chris Rogers in a pub opposite the studios of ITN where he worked as a presenter on ITV News. I had known Chris since he was a teenager and on his first assignment with the BBC. Like me, Chris had been moved by Shay's photograph of Rosie and a deal was sealed with a handshake and a pint of Guinness, though he still had to pitch the proposal to his bosses at ITV News.

I reported back to Shay and he agreed that he would smuggle the journalists into the jails, and Hazel was first in working covertly with a secret weapon: her camera. After Hazel, Father Shay helped Chris and a cameraman from ITV News to film undercover inside the jails. The footage both journalists captured was shocking. Afterwards, Chris told me, "The filming conditions were the most horrific I've experienced; the stench inside the cells was pretty unbearable."

We launched our campaign in August 2005 when ITV News made *Kids Behind Bars* their lead story, and their top presenter, Michael Mates, faced the television cameras with our 86-page report clutched in his hand. Viewers deluged ITV News and we were told that the switchboard crashed at one point.

Alongside the television coverage, Hazel's dispatch to the international media with her stunning photographs captured the grim pathos of life inside Filipino jails:

I saw children detained in overcrowded prisons and uninhabitable conditions. In flooded and damp cells, with little light, stifling heat and no fresh air, the children's health was affected. Many children had skin conditions after being months, even years, in these conditions. I witnessed children covered in ring worm and scabies, their skin looking aged by disease with one boy's face covered by infected boils. The most shocking sight was a jail in Metro Manila. Within a cell measuring 1 metre by 5 metres, we found two children among the thirteen people in this tiny, inhumane space, crammed in like animals. I have seen a dog kennel, housing just one dog, bigger than the space that housed these thirteen adults and children. One of the prisons I gained access to had dirty river water, which came halfway up my shins, across the whole floor area of the jail. The children in the prison were in the darkest cell at the far end of the jail. Kids squeezed together on a table; the youngest crouched on the floor in the water looking depressed. I learnt that the flooding was a daily occurrence. There was a stench of stale body odour and urine, which in the humidity became unbearable. I heard that one of the youngest imprisoned was a child of nine. Most are illegally detained for trivial offences and many are held on mere suspicion with long delays in the justice process. The youngest are often subjected to sexual abuse by the guards and other prisoners; girls are most at risk. The cells are packed full, with prisoners taking turns to sleep on the concrete floor while others stand. Inmates pay to stand beside the fan to cool off from the fierce heat. Disease spreads quickly and the children are the most vulnerable. They are weak and malnourished with their daily food allowance being only 33 peso (about 30 pence). Enduring intense heat, lack of ventilation, little exercise or recreation, having to squat on the floor twenty-four hours a day causes physical and mental breakdown. They live in fear of bullying and beatings by guards and inmates.

Alongside the media coverage, thousands of postcards went flying out, hundreds of copies of our report were sent to relevant authorities, supporters collected thousands of petitions to the UN, which were stacked up over a foot high in the office. The pressure intensified with a hearing before the US Congress organized by Ann Buwalda in Washington and chaired by Congressmen Christopher Smith and Joseph Pitts. ITV's television report was screened and Chris Rogers flew over to testify along with David Alton and Father Shay.

Our strategic objective was to use the media to report that kids were trapped in an international blind spot, and Chris's television report summed things up: "These broadcasts were what the world was not meant to see."

The Filipino government sent out encouraging signals but we weren't holding our breath. Six months later Chris and an ITV film crew jetted back to the Philippines and once again Father Shay smuggled them in. Chris's article on ITV's website captured the drama:

The images of hundreds of child prisoners held in horrendously overcrowded jails sent shockwaves around the globe. Six months later, I returned to see what had changed – only to discover another scandal. Prison cell after prison cell of broken lives and broken promises. We found young faces still behind bars, hungry, exhausted and terrified. The children were stacked like farm animals on to shelves three stories high. There wasn't enough room to stand up and even sitting down they had to crouch. As I handed out food, I felt like I was feeding caged animals. As we walked through another prison, the number of young hands reaching out to me was overwhelming. We met twelve-year-old

Sarah, accused of shoplifting. She told me the door to the female cell is left open and male prisoners have harassed her. It would cost her parents a month's wages to bail her out.

CNN picked up ITV's broadcast and again the story received worldwide coverage and created a stir in the Philippines. Hazel Thompson's prison images won several coveted awards including first prize in the *Observer*'s Hodge competition. One of the judges, Kirsty Wark from BBC 2's *Newsnight*, said, "It's a remarkable image. It's something special in journalistic terms as well, because these children are in an adult jail. The fact that places like this exist in the twenty-first century is extraordinary. The set of pictures captures something out of the horror of a Hieronymus Bosch or Brueghel painting."

Some people thought the campaign had been effective. We'd had excellent political support, obtained great media coverage, and run out of campaign materials, requiring an immediate reprint. But this wasn't satisfying. How could it be? Our objective was to change the law to stop children from being jailed with adults.

Change at last

The breakthrough finally came in April 2006, when President Arroyo signed the bill known as Republic Act 9344, a turning point in the Filipino juvenile justice system. As a result of this new law, 70 per cent of criminal cases against children would be dismissed completely. Children would no longer be jailed and kids under fifteen years would be sent to youth homes instead. Finally, we had the result we wanted.

Father Shay identified land in the countryside for a new boys' home. He told me, "It's ideal for a working farm and vocation training centre but we need funds to start it and keep it going."

He explained that this new home would be open to children like Edwin:

Arriving at Preda's Children's Home, on the Upper Kalaklan Heights, Edwin came to a little kingdom of heaven on the hillside, overlooking the azure waters of Subic Bay. Below are the glistening beaches where Edwin, and fifty-seven former child prisoners like him, can run free and play. As each day passes, they discover their childhood. They are building sandcastles and splashing in the surf to their heart's content. He can now read, write, and use a computer for the first time in his life.

We knew that the problem wasn't over and that Shay would have to be vigilant and monitor the jails in the future to ensure that the law was upheld. Still it felt good to know that our campaign had succeeded in its objective to change the law.

But Father Shay joked that he would pay the price of success: "The kids will not now go to jail but to homes like ours. The government is not building any!"

CHAPTER 15

Tsunami Memories

Catamarans for Survivors, 2004–05

With one sudden torrential explosion "tsunami" invaded our lexicon of consciousness in December 2004, becoming one of those rare words that is understood in any language. It claimed over 200,000 lives in thirteen countries and registered a 9.15 magnitude, which made it the third largest earthquake ever recorded on a seismograph.

Until that day I couldn't have explained what a tsunami was or did. Even the fishermen I met in Pondicherry later told me that they had never heard the word before that fatal December morning.

When the tsunami struck on the 26th, I was safe at home. As the epic scale of the tragedy unfolded, I assumed that all I could do was to write a cheque to the Disasters Emergency Committee (DEC) and trust that it would do some good for someone somewhere.

The name "tsunami" comes from two Japanese words: "tsu" means "port" and "nami" means "wave". Because of its location, more undersea earthquakes impact Japan than anywhere else in the world and $20 million annually was spent on early warning systems.

Scientists reported that the impact of the 2004 tsunami caused the earth's surface to move vertically up to about 1 cm. The tsunami wave moved at 500 mph under the sea and rose to 100 feet high in some places. The epicentre of the undersea earthquake was in northern Sumatra and the nearby city of Banda Aceh was almost completely destroyed in about 15 minutes. Curiously, this was almost exactly one year (to the hour) after a 6.6 magnitude earthquake killed an estimated 30,000 people in the ancient city of Bam in Iran.

I was intrigued by stories I'd heard that animals were alert to the coming devastation. Another fisherman nodded and told me, "Yes, buffaloes, goats and dogs survived because they fled." In the Andaman Islands, the Stone Age community were alerted by the behaviour of their animals' instinct for survival and followed them to safety. In Bang Koey, Thailand, a herd of buffalo grazing by the beach suddenly lifted up their heads, ears standing upright, looked out to sea, turned, and stampeded up the hill, followed by bewildered villagers whose lives were thereby saved. This scene was repeated in Sri Lanka and Sumatra. Elephants have special bones in their feet enabling them to sense seismic vibrations before we can. Wildlife experts in Sri Lanka expressed surprise that they found no evidence of large-scale animal deaths, indicating that they may have sensed the imminent danger and fled to higher ground.

Aftermath

I telephoned my friend, Dr Wai Sin Hu, in India, and learned that his organization, Samaritan's Helps, knew families who had been hit hard. His workers were on the spot and could act swiftly but had no resources. All they needed was help and I pledged some backing.

The tsunami moved everyone to action. The news media reported that this was the greatest outpouring of global generosity responding to the worst natural disaster in human history. In the UK, 91 per cent of Britons together donated an unprecedented £350 million, distributed by the DEC to twelve large charities. I knew that we could never compete with these big groups but was assured that we could directly help specific families who had lost everything. Almost at once, people stepped up. The Surrey Chamber of Commerce backed our appeal, Gary Brooker, founder of the band Procul Harum and the writer of "A Whiter Shade of Pale", played a benefit concert at Guildford Cathedral, and Survivor Records organized over 250 gospel artists who recorded a charity single ("One Voice, One Heart") for us at the Abbey Road studios.

Our friends at Samaritan's Helps advised us that our funds should be spent on the construction of homes, and to provide catamarans and nets for fisherman in a village called Thantri, a small hamlet of sixty families tucked along India's east coast near Pondicherry.

It should have been straightforward. The area had been devastated. The funds had been raised. We had a trusted partner. Yet, it was all moving slowly and had become complex. I wanted to find out why things were delayed, so about one year later, accompanied by my son Luke, aged sixteen, we set off to investigate.

The town of Pondicherry had an easy-going breezy feel to it, and locals proudly declared that the coastline was the second longest beach in the world, though no one was sure which was the first. The town traced its history and trade connections with Rome to 100 BC and to Greece in AD 100. Amid bustling streets and chugging traffic, its French heritage was still in evidence in cobbled streets, neatly laid roads, wide promenades, architecturally imposing churches, and statues of Joan of Arc. Commemorative festivals were held regularly at which retired soldiers still paraded and sang both the Indian and French national anthems.

Fishing in Pondicherry had been a way of life for thousands of years. Classic poems celebrated the life of a fisherman, just like that of Dara Varadaryan in Thantri, whose house was about 100 strides from the beach. Dara, a man of dignity, stood tall, as he told us his story.

Like his father before him, Dara rose before dawn each day, signed on for a local fishing boat owner, and sailed with some of the able-bodied men from this quaint fishing village. Over the years, his ancestors had relied on the sea for their livelihood but with polluted waters, mounting restrictions, and an increasing number of fishing vessels, the old days were fading and times growing hard. The haul of crabs, prawns, shrimp, and small fish that they caught were sold in the local bazaar and the profits shared out. Half went to the owner of the vessel, the boat's diesel was paid out of the other half, and anything left over would be split among the crew of three to six men. Before the tsunami, Dara's share of the takings on some days was down to 15 rupees, barely 10p. The future seemed bleak for this sea labourer and his family. "But what can I do?" Dara asked, speaking through an interpreter. "Fishing is my life."

Dara spoke with controlled emotion when he remembered the day that terror came to Thantri. The tsunami made no sound; in stealth, like a silent invader, the angry sea rose and advanced towards the shore with a sudden deadly force.

He could hardly believe the sight before him. "The sea was about 10 to 12 feet high. There were no waves that caused the sea to rise. It was just this huge terrifying wall of sea coming towards us. I had never seen anything like it. As far as the eye could see," he told us, stretching his hand across the horizon, "Everywhere..."

All around there was chaos in Thantri. No one knew what was happening, what to expect, or what to do. "We thought the world was coming to an end," the fisherman explained.

Dara grabbed his wife and young son and they ran as fast as they could away from the seashore. Within minutes, the village had emptied, each villager clutching what they could, running blind, seeking higher ground.

Amid the turmoil, a young child had been left behind and was playing on the beach, directly in the path of the tsunami. Incredibly, the first force scooped the child onto the roof of the sea wall and hurtled him forward; he landed deep inside the village, bruised but safe.

South Asia's coastline was devastated by the undersea earthquake that created the monster tidal wave which smashed into seaside towns and villages. The stories have been documented and become part of our collective memory.

In Thantri, as in other places, after the initial blast the sea vanished from sight, about 300 metres in some places, and the floor of the actual seabed was visible. Live fish were stranded on the shore and household belongings spread out across the open sand. Spotting the opportunity but not the danger, villagers rushed back to retrieve personal items and to take advantage of the fish floundering on the beach. Sadly, all those who did so died, as the huge wall of sea returned in a second lethal strike.

More damage was done by the receding waves because of the suction and pressure, and evidence was clearly visible strewn throughout the village when we visited. Bits of catamaran lay at the side of the road far from the beach, uprooted trees rested where they had fallen, and elsewhere branches and shrubs lay wasted, alongside rubble from houses that had collapsed. The debris remained untended, a visual memorial of that December day.

"I still wake in the middle of the night and wonder when the tsunami might return," Dara confessed. His words were endorsed by the other fishermen and they nodded their head in unison. "We live in fear of that terrible day," one old man said.

Beginning to rebuild

When the fishermen learned that Luke and I represented individuals and groups who had provided the catamarans and nets, their appreciation was spontaneous and sincere. One man said, "We lost everything and were destitute. We didn't know what would happen to our families and our children." Another added, "We are so grateful for the catamarans and the nets. Each day this strengthens us. Because of this help we have started to rebuild our community."

Dara agreed, and thanked us. He stood proudly by his new catamaran and stroked the side of the vessel. While some groups have distributed larger, diesel-driven, fibreglass boats, he said that the traditional wooden sailing craft, like those employed by his ancestors, was a wiser choice. He explained, "The fibreglass boats are costlier to run and expensive to repair; they can lose money if the fishing is bad as each day the run must first pay for the trip's diesel." Another fisherman added, "The catamarans are flexible, reliable, long-lasting, easy to use, and they are more profitable."

Dara shook his head in affirmation. His income had risen 100 per cent from 15 rupees a day to 150 rupees. He was no longer dependent on the local fishing trade but had been able to start building a sustainable future for his family. The same was true of the other fishermen in the community who had received our catamarans.

We were introduced to two widows of fishermen who died, as each had received one of our catamarans. The widows had appointed caretakers, fishermen who took charge of the vessels and then split the proceeds of the sale with the women. It was evidence of care and common purpose within the community.

We were shown the fishing nets that our donations had bought and these were clearly of importance to the fishermen. There were ten main types of nets with thirteen variations of these, each designed for a particular type of catch. Intricately woven, a handmade net that weighed 5 kilograms would take about a week to ten days to complete and such valuable tools were closely inspected after each day at sea.

The news had spread along the costal route, and Thantri had attracted interest from other villages because of the speed with which it had renewed its community.

Red tape

Dara's house was on the beach, just about a hundred paces from the seashore, an idyllic spot that you'd expect to see on the cover of a holiday brochure. An occasional ship was sighted on the turquoise sea.

He grew up on this beach and was taught the significance of the tide and the secrets of the fishing trade by his father. One day, he assumed, he would pass that tradition on to his son. Dara's house, like many others, is a concrete structure, and though damaged, was patched up and made habitable for temporary accommodation. But the location of his property and others in this village was mired in controversy and confusion. As with numerous conflicts around the world, the issue was land.

After our partner had successfully completed the provision of catamarans and nets for tsunami survivors in this local fishing community in Pondicherry, local government officials gave us an undertaking that we could begin the reconstruction of homes for Dara and fishermen like him. Our partner had meetings, reports of meetings, and assurances of further meetings. But progress was slow, and I had travelled to Pondicherry assuming that my visit would illuminate the puzzling situation. How hard could it be?

The government's case was explained to me: "The fishermen must leave their present home and sign the property over to the authorities. In return, they would be provided with alternative accommodation."

But fishermen like Dara were hesitant and argued, "This new land won't be in our names. It's far from the beach and located in the interior of the village. We live on the beach. We wake up before dawn and it's easy to get into our boats and go fishing. What will happen to our catamarans at night if we don't live on the beach?"

The local officials were adamant that the fishermen could live on the new land for as long as they wished. But I could tell from the faces of the fisherman that not everyone believed the politicians' assurances. "We have promised to compensate everyone for the land they give up on the beach," the official insisted.

"At what rate?" Dara asked.

"We'll let you know the rate after everyone has relocated," the bureaucrat replied.

As I sat in a stuffy office and contemplated the deal, I could understand the fishermen's suspicion. Why couldn't a reasonable resolution be found that acknowledged the needs of the fishermen who had already suffered so much?

For Dara, it meant leaving his ancestral home and moving from the beach, clearly a prime location and vital for his trade as a fisherman. It was an exceptionally beautiful spot, and I sympathized with him. I didn't feel confident encouraging him to leave his home on the promise of a politician without being told what compensation he would receive. Could we really trust the authorities in this somewhat complex land deal? And who would occupy Dara's land after he had vacated the property?

Our own transactions with the local government had become entangled. At first I was relieved when they signed an agreement with us in April 2005, stipulating that each house we built would cost 70,000 rupees (about £890), and tried to push this through immediately. But in June, new "guidelines" were published. The cost of each house had risen – in fact, doubled in cost – to 175,000 rupees (£1,900). The new rules set out the exact size and details of the property to be built, insisting that once work started it must be completed in three months' time. Our partner complained, "How is this going to be possible? Building materials are in short supply."

Although no money goes directly to the government for the reconstruction and rebuilding work, it was they alone who could grant permission to rebuild. When it was clear that our partner wouldn't be forced into a deal, the local administration passed our allocation to another organization who had agreed to the new costs. This was a blow and I was disappointed.

Mixed in this milieu and moving in stealth were would-be politicians, trying to make a name for themselves, ingratiating themselves with the fishermen, while seeking to elevate their role and influence, succeeding mainly in generating heat and dust.

I found my head swirling. It was deeply frustrating to be so near a resolution but unable to influence the intransigence of the authorities. I wanted to push on with the construction but our partner cautioned against it. It turned out to be wise counsel.

Not one brick was laid on any house in Thantri by the other group, the plot of land set aside for the building work remained empty, and somehow the fishermen got by. Little changed, except the house costs, which spiralled upwards to 200,000 rupees (£2,500) per house, considerably more than their original quote of 70,000 rupees (£890).

I learned that there were similar unresolved issues along the coast from Pondicherry to Chennai, and, digging deeper, I discovered that in Banda Aceh itself, the epicentre of the earthquake, the reconstruction had been hampered by the conflict between the Indonesian military and rebels fighting for independence, a conflict that had claimed the lives of 12,000 individuals, mostly civilians.

It was the same in Thailand, where the race to rebuild the infrastructure in familiar tourist resorts before the holiday season had fallen behind schedule. By August 2005, eight months after the earthquake, only two Phuket beaches, Patong and Kamala, were back to normal as local businessmen increased pressure on the authorities to spend its 1.1 billion baht budget on infrastructure and tourism. Tourism in Phuket accounted for roughly 30 per cent of Thailand's overall GDP and thousands relied on the tourist industry to sustain their livelihood.

While the tsunami took everyone by surprise, it was disappointing that more was not accomplished and it was hard to reconcile the conflicts that had arisen that seemed to overwhelm the simple objective of helping people in need. These were huge organizations that controlled vast amounts of money donated, and yet on the ground, it was disheartening to see just how slowly things moved. In our case, I knew we were in good hands with our partners, who would not take a step back until our mission had been completed, but I wondered what would happen to the tsunami survivors after the television cameras had turned to the next big disaster.

The "Untouchables"

Before leaving, Luke and I toured the local area. Pondicherry's idyllic backwaters were enchanting and tranquil, with groves of coconut palms swaying gracefully amid the gentle flowing waters of a hidden lagoon. Cool sea breezes from the beach were a constant reminder of the nearby shore leading to the turquoise sea. Secluded from the city, such near-secret hideaways would easily compete with any remote tropical island in the sun, and I imagined bringing Joan and the family here sometime.

On the day we visited, there were very few people to be seen but I spotted a near-naked figure of a fisherman wading through the lagoon. He'd sling his raggedy net into the water and then wade through, one weary step at a time. He told us his name was Karthgayam. His leathery skin was battered and worn and hung slackly on his wiry frame of seventy-four years. Each day he walked the few yards from his tiny hut to this sleepy lagoon and prepared for another day under the hot, blistering sun. He'd been here from dawn, and since the tsunami struck, his life had followed this monotonous routine.

Before the disaster, he owned a catamaran with five different types of nets, and as a fisherman, had raised ten children. But the years had not been kind. In his village, there were eighty-five men like him who had once had catamarans but only fourteen were left; his own vessel was lost in the storm, along with his nets; somehow he managed to salvage three nets and repair them. His children have grown and gone; now with only his elderly wife for companionship, life was a struggle. With no one to turn to, he did the only thing he knew, and returned to the sea.

Each day he rose early and returned to this backwater to wade through the lagoon; he relied on his nets but also his hands to catch something, anything. At day's end, his wife would take his catch to the local market and from this sale they bought their food. "Sometimes, it's 50 rupees (about 60p) but mostly it's about 20 rupees (nearly 25p). It's not enough to feed us."

On the afternoon we visited Pondicherry, Karthgayam had been in the water for several hours. "Can you show us your catch?" I asked him.

He held three tiny shrimp in the palm of his hand and looked directly at me. "I've been here all day. This is what I have."

Karthgayam was part of a particular fishing community that had been ignored and I discovered that, nearly one year after the tragedy, they were hidden victims who had received no help from the outside world.

When the boundary was redrawn in Pondicherry, this hamlet fell outside the scope of the geographical divide and consequently they had no representation in the political system. The old MLA (Member of the Legislative Assembly) wasn't interested in them because they wouldn't vote for him, and the community didn't know who would be elected to represent their area so they had no one to contact. They had no "vote banks" as they are called; neither did they have anyone to organize the group. "No one hears our voice," one member explained. "As a result we have not received any help."

Karthgayam, and everyone else in the village like him, was a Dalit. Dalits or "Untouchables" comprise about 250 million people, the lowest in India's Hindu caste system. Caste discrimination is forbidden by the Indian constitution, but the law was rarely enforced by the police and the courts. India's Dalits – a Sanskrit word meaning "crushed" or "downtrodden" – have been oppressed for over three centuries. A person stays in the same caste from birth to death and this rank is handed down from generation to generation. "It's their karma," someone explained to me, trying to be helpful. "It's a belief that status in life is decided by deeds in a previous life." The caste system is an integral part of Indian society and deeply ingrained in the Indian perspective.

* * *

It was an unusual experience and a privilege to visit tsunami villages and to meet fishermen who faced the storm and survived. But it was also frustrating to be entrapped in the bureaucratic red tape that stalled the rebuilding of homes for the fishermen. I was confident that we were in safe hands with Samaritan's Helps, and eventually they succeeded in rebuilding homes for the fishermen in Thantri – late, but completed. Our partner's integrity ensured that our money was spent wisely and not squandered or diverted, and that we served the best interests of the fishermen and their families in Thantri. Their tact with handling government regulations and officials ensured that our independence was maintained and that our funds were directed to those for whom our support was intended: tsunami survivors.

By the time we were ready to leave Pondicherry, I was feeling unsettled. The experience of meeting Karthgayam had disturbed me. I would never forget this solitary figure who posed a tragic form against a landscape of breathtaking beauty.

CHAPTER 16

Defining Issues of the Twenty-First Century

Putting a Stop to Child Porn and Human Trafficking, 1992–present

When I sat in front of my first computer, I pressed a few buttons and was pleasantly surprised at how thoughtful the inventors had been. Ah, I sighed, even a place for my coffee cup, as the CD drive slid out.

I've been enticed by new media but without the touch of a physical hand to be my digital guide, I sometimes viewed the latest must-have techno-whizzo-gizmos with suspicion and intrigue. Eventually, when discovered in electric sunshine, I turned to my kids: Jessica selected my first mobile phone, Rachel taught me how to text, and it is Luke whom I've called on to fix my Skype phone.

I didn't embark on a GPS device until 2007 because I confidently predicted that I wouldn't be able to use it, and was nudged, or rather shoved, into it by Father Shay Cullen. This was after a journey to Bath, which encompassed an unintentional tour of the city, while seeking the venue for his meeting that evening. We eventually made contact with the organizers through the employment of a mobile phone, and a scouting party was dispatched to locate us. Father Shay's parting words to me were, "I'm not getting in the car with you again until you buy a satellite navigation system!" I decided to take his advice (not for the first time!) and our TomTom was purchased over the internet.

The internet has been described as the end of not knowing everything. It's one of the greatest inventions of our times. The benefits and the possibilities, of course, are beyond imagination. How can one explain that sleek slithers of gloriously designed gadgets can hold hundreds of books and thousands of songs? Or that forty-eight hours of video are uploaded onto YouTube every minute? If Facebook were a country, it would be the world's third largest and twice the size of the US population.

While researching the issue of slavery, I discovered ebooks, and became a fan. I was able to obtain obscure texts and materials on the slave trade, buy them cheaply, and store them with ease, since they were on CDs. They contained voluminous information and put them within easy reach. Hard copies would have been difficult to obtain and expensive.

The wizardry of new technology has changed the world we know and influenced the way we act. Activists and campaigners have seized the day and ignited the landscape, blazing a pathway forward with courage and Twitter. The glow from the viral video electronic bush fire turned the dreaded Joseph Kony into an invisible war criminal on the run in Uganda. Twitter and Facebook were used to great effect during the "Arab Spring". One of our recent campaigns captured global interest, and people in over ninety countries signed our online petition. The global reach of the internet connected us and enabled people to express their outrage alongside their activism.

Cyber attack, Philippines, 2009

But it wasn't just activists that embraced new technology. UN experts warned that child pornography online was increasing despite attempts to curb it. This was a global crime in cyberspace and the internet has become the international medium for the spread of child porn. Anonymous, the anarchic cyber-guerrilla network, not dissimilar to WikiLeaks, has been called a digital Robin Hood. In 2011, they hacked into a porn ring, published the names of 1,500 people who used "Lolita-City", and took down forty websites that stored 100 gigabytes of child porn. But there's no end in sight, and porn rings have been exposed with depressing consistency.

Father Shay alerted us that child porn DVDs were available "under the counter" of most street-side vendors in the Philippines and other Asian countries. Shay told me:

> Young lives are being damaged in the production of this vile material, while others corrupted and led into sex acts with young children after viewing the material. Such images are evidence of crimes against children and that's why in all civilized countries where the rule of law prevails, child pornography is anathema, and violators get lengthy prison sentences.

But not yet in the Philippines.

It was simply astonishing to learn – in 2009 – that there was no specific law to block child pornography in the Philippines, a country known for attracting sex tourists. Shay explained:

> Thousands have been arrested worldwide for downloading such illegal images but the server corporations make billions of dollars out of facilitating this evil trade. That's the one reason they do not want to install anti-child porn filters and set up an independent monitoring group that finds the source and either blocks the offending website or helps police identify the offenders.

With Shay we started our research with the Internet Watch Foundation in Cambridge, where they showed us the technology they used to monitor websites suspected of promoting child porn. Later, we met with Christian Sjöberg, an activist-turned-entrepreneur in Sweden, who developed Netclean WhiteBox technology for internet service providers to block websites containing abusive material. It was supported by Interpol and implemented in New Zealand. Despite issues of censorship advanced by some, Christian told us, "The technology is available to stop the spread of child porn." As a result, we launched a campaign in 2009 together with Shay to establish a law to ban child pornography in the Philippines. Our focus was to get the authorities to speed up a bill that was languishing in the Filipino legal system. Shay's article published worldwide outlined the objectives of our campaign: "The new law must make blocking mandatory for all. Voluntary self-regulations should never be a substitute for the law. We need that law urgently. It will save children from abuse and will help us rescue and give them a new start in life."

Our supporters were great, shooting letters and emails to the Filipino authorities, including the President, Mrs Gloria Macapagal-Arroyo. If a reply came, it was usually from a political underling couched in predictable diplomatic jargon: "We're doing everything we can... These things take time..."

The Filipino President never replied. She was busy preparing for a visit to Washington. Mrs Arroyo had been honoured as the first Southeast Asian leader invited by the newly elected American President Barrack Obama to visit the White House. Their afternoon meeting on 30 July 2009 was relaxed and the "photo op" clearly bolstered Mrs Arroyo's status at home.

Three days before her meeting with President Obama in Washington, she was passed a letter by American Congressman Trent Franks, an Arizona Republican, who had supported our Kids Behind Bars campaign and backed our new project. His message to President Arroyo said:

> *Just as hundreds of street children experienced sexual abuse*
> *and mistreatment when illegally imprisoned with adults before*
> *the passage of the Juvenile Justice Bill, the abuse of children*

in the child pornography industry is equally distressing and unconscionable in today's world. I remain deeply concerned with the thousands of children whose lives are destroyed on a daily basis by the abuse related to the child pornography industry, and I am heartened to know that Parliament is trying to address this serious problem.

The timing couldn't have been better. Would President Arroyo's delegation be mindful of a US politician's concerns, and push this bill up the queue? We didn't have long to wait.

Four months later, in November, President Arroyo signed the new anti-child pornography bill into law. It was a first step, but an important one. The new law was hard-hitting and made the display and distribution of child porn illegal – in any form. It was one of the first laws in the world that required internet service providers (ISPs) to install filtering software to block access to websites that show abusive images of children.

The industry has rejected the enforcement of filtering software and warned that government snooping and surveillance is an invasion of privacy; even the UK favours a voluntary approach. But Shay argued:

There is no total and absolute right over anything or anybody in the world. If the freedom of action of some is harming and allowing the abuse of others, especially children, then action must be taken to protect the vulnerable and the victimized. One right must not be used to violate another right. All of us have a responsibility to protect children and bring violators to justice. Industry has a social responsibility to make their services child-safe just like any other product. They must put children before profits.

This new law isn't a magic bullet. It's not going to wipe out every grisly image and loathsome website where children are tortured and abused. But the global reach of child porn can't be left to corporations and ISPs to resolve or curb. Government authorities should intervene, and law enforcement take action. The campaign to push through the first anti-child porn law in the Philippines taught us that we didn't need to be a techno wizard to become a cyber warrior.

Sex trafficking in the Philippines

I became aware of modern slavery in 1992, on my first day in the Philippines. I learned that young girls were trafficked to Japan by criminal gangs with links to the Yakuza (Japanese mafia). The gangs used recruiters, frequently women, who enticed girls with fake promises of a job and a better life, with money for their family.

Over the years Father Shay rescued many girls after being tipped off that they were to be trafficked out of the country. He knew of trafficking routes into Europe, and told me of one young girl who had been trafficked to London. She had written to her mother in the Philippines, and he had become aware of the letter.

Modern-day slavery is a secret perilous world. Yesterday's slavers and slave traders have become today's sex tourists and traffickers. The slaving ships and clippers have gone; now it's jets and laptops as they cross the planet using the twenty-first-century technology of mobile phones and the internet. They target the dispossessed and powerless, the weak and vulnerable, those who have been born into poverty and whose lives are trapped in a vicious chain of debt. Many are teenagers, just like the twins Jean and Mia in the Philippines. Father Shay documented their story:

> *Jean and Mia were twins, born of a father they never knew, raised by a mother who didn't care, who sold them off to a pimp when only fourteen years old. They were raped in a sex bar the following week. I heard about their abduction and started an investigation.*
>
> *It was a large glittering façade that greeted me as I went inside looking for the teenagers. I had received a tip-off and was*

sure they were here. In the foyer a man dressed in black and bedecked with gold chains and sparkling diamond rings was the trafficker and slaver of children. He looked the part.

I was greeted as a potential customer with smiles and laughter. "Have a good time, Joe!" the mamasan gushed and ushered me in.

Inside the club, the girls paraded as they were taught. They looked sad and sultry, caged and cringing, behind the make-up and the mascara. This was the modern-day auction. No more the wharf-side platform lined with disembarked wrecks of suffering slaves cringing beneath the blows and whips of the slave seller. Now we had soft lights and music, and the even softer sell.

The trafficking of children and women is growing. I discovered Filipino children as young as nine to sixteen turned into child prostitutes in backstreets and bars of Angeles and Olongapo, Manila and Bulacan, Malinta and Cebu. They are trafficked to Japan, Korea, South Africa, Asia, and the Middle East. Countries like the Philippines have a low rate of HIV/AIDS and so women and minors from these places are much in demand. That's why many sex tourists prefer the Philippines above other sex-industry destinations.

There is no need nowadays for the slave hunters to storm the villages with musket, cutlass, rope, and net. The recruiters and traffickers lure the youth with payments and promises of good jobs, but they end up prisoners of exploitation and abuse. Even jobs abroad are dangled before parents, and cash payments and promises seal the deal, and the life of a village girl is damaged and destroyed, the hope of an education gone; a childhood is stolen, dreams are crushed.

I found neither Jean nor Mia that night but picked up another tip that they were going to be sent abroad. Before that could happen, Jean had had enough abuse and slipped away and went back to her mother, who was part of the deal. She did nothing to rescue Mia, who was slated to be shipped out and sold off in Japan, where about 35,000 Filipino women and minors are trafficked into the "entertainment" industry every year. Pressure is mounting on the Japanese to crack down on this trafficking that masquerades as "visiting entertainers".

I found Jean back in Olongapo and she told me where her sister was being held. I brought Preda's social workers, her mother, and the police to the den, and we found twenty young women, of whom several appeared to be teenagers, and her sister Mia was among the captives.

Soon two pimps showed up with a man and a woman. The man was the same one in black and gold chains that I had seen in the sex club. He was furious. The woman was shouting abuse at the police. It was tense and dangerous and I thought he would pull out a gun. He demanded that the police should radio for their superiors. It was clear that he had paid off someone. The police I had with me were from another unit. They stayed outside, showing no interest to begin an investigation; instead they began to discuss what looked like a pay off.

I went into the house, saw and photographed a list of names and flights to Japan. Then I got Mia out of the house and into the van and we drove off. I only wish I could have rescued the others.

Back at the Preda Home, both teenagers settled in quickly, and during the emotional expression therapy, they cried and screamed, pouring out all their anger and hurt at their mother for selling them, at the abuser for raping them, and crying out, "Why did it happen?" They relived the abuse but this time they had the confidence to open up. Their long-buried pain came pouring out and they were into the healing process; eventually they recovered. But it was dangerous as the traffickers had threatened to shoot their mother if they filed charges. Today, both sisters are enrolled in junior college.

From 1996 onwards I regularly heard first-hand stories of teenage girls who were trafficked from Nepal into India, but also trafficked internally. The girls had been rescued by Reverend Devaraj, and each one had their own story to tell. The route from Nepal to India was controlled by criminal gangs who enforced their rule by violence. But some girls had been sold by their husbands or tricked by their friends, even family members.

Sex trafficking usually catches the headlines and the cases of exploited young girls have been the subject of dramas and documentaries. In Britain, Operation Pentameter (in 2006 and 2007) brought together all police forces into a co-operative effort to get an understanding of sex slavery in Britain. Their investigation uncovered trafficking rings that delivered thousands of girls and women into Britain. Many were East European youth desperate for jobs. It was known that slave auctions were held at Stansted Airport in 2006, with girls taken directly to British brothels. Yet the numbers involved in sex trafficking (and other forms of slavery) were insignificant when compared to the statistics of slaves trafficked into debt bondage.

Slavery in the twenty-first century

Bonded labour is the most common form of modern slavery and affects about 20 million people worldwide, according to the UN's Working Group on Contemporary Forms of Slavery. In *Disposable People: New Slavery in the Global Economy* (2009), Kevin Bales writes that India "may have more slaves than all the other countries of the world put together", with the majority of slaves in India being Dalits or "Untouchables" – like the fisherman I met after the tsunami. Dalits comprise nearly one-quarter of India's society and constitute the largest number of people who have been categorized as modern-day slaves in any single nation on earth.

Slavery has existed throughout human history. In ancient cultures, slaves were often prisoners of war, but the enslaved were not defined by colour or race; many were European. The transatlantic slave trade transformed all this. It became the largest international business of the age, and the world was changed beyond anything anyone could comprehend.

The slaves of Africa were central to the new world order as they provided the labour force that was the engine for this new international financial system. No one was untouched by the institution of slavery, and it has become central to an understanding of our world today. Simply, the transatlantic slave trade enriched and developed every slave trading country, and the wealth of European and American nations has come largely from the sweat of slaves.

The transatlantic slave trade ended for several reasons. The slave trade was no longer the reliable and lucrative investment it had once been; the revolts and uprisings among the slaves themselves increased and spread fear. Pressure came from the campaign mounted by the abolitionist movement led by Thomas Clarkson, starting with the Quakers and church groups, widely supported by women, and reinforced by African slaves themselves, men such as Olaudah Equiano. William Wilberforce led the Parliamentary campaign and spurred other politicians to action.

Slavery is illegal in every country on our planet, yet there are more slaves alive today than all the slaves stolen from Africa over four centuries of the slave trade. Kevin Bales, one of the leading authorities on modern slavery, estimates that there are 27 million slaves in the world today – a shocking, haunting statistic.

The global panorama of the twenty-first-century slave trade affects every continent of the world. Human trafficking has been described as the buying, selling, and transporting of people for exploitation and abuse, controlled by coercion and force. It has become the fastest growing and the second most profitable transnational crime worldwide. Globalization has made it easier for traffickers to move "product" around the world, while revolutionary changes in technology and politics have had a huge impact on the movement of money, goods, and people.

Analysts have given these reasons for the booming business: the collapse of Russian communism and the end of the Cold War has seen a growth in trafficking with reduced internal border controls; the increase of organized crime and regional conflicts; while a mass global migration has caused an estimated 190 million (in 2005) to live outside their country of birth.

In *Human Trafficking: A Global Perspective* (2010), Lousie Shelley notes:

> *Today, trafficking is truly a global phenomenon. Many countries are simultaneously source, transit and destination countries for trafficking. Despite the disproportionate attention to sex trafficking today, contemporary trafficking victims are more likely to be victims of labour trafficking, forced to serve as child soldiers, or trapped in domestic servitude.*

In 2002 Jubilee Campaign lobbied the UK government to tackle trafficking and called for new laws against this modern form of slavery, and asked supporters to petition the government. At the time, no comprehensive legislation existed to cover people who were trafficked into the UK, where their abductors held them captive and controlled all their funds.

Our campaign's first success occurred that year, when the Home Office minister Beverley Hughes formally responded to us and said that the government would create a new offence for trafficking (for prostitution) within the Nationality, Immigration and Asylum Bill, and further legislation (in line with the EU) would be introduced to curb labour and sexual exploitation. We didn't get everything we wanted but it was a start and evidence that we'd made an impact with our petition. The same year, 2002, David Alton initiated one of the first full debates on trafficking, calling for new laws to prevent trafficking, and wrote to encourage our supporters:

It is always a positive step to have prompted the Government to respond to specific points of action that we have raised. We are delighted at the number of supporters who have taken action – this is proof that ordinary people can make their voices heard. We welcome the Government's stated intention to introduce new legislation on this issue in the next Queen's Speech. We will be holding them to account for this pledge.

Over the next decade, the issue was raised by Parliamentarians and activists backed by widespread media coverage, and as a result, a greater awareness of modern-day slavery has emerged. Before retiring from Parliament, former MP Anthony Steen introduced the Anti-Slavery Day Bill and it became law in 2010. This legislation in Parliament defined modern-day slavery as child trafficking, forced labour, domestic servitude, and trafficking for sexual exploitation. Parliament declared 18 October as "Anti-Slavery Day", and it would serve to raise awareness of modern slavery and to inspire people to end it.

The Human Trafficking Foundation

Anthony made plans to set up the Human Trafficking Foundation and David Alton asked me to help; in turn, I drew in Bill Hampson. It was Bill who had first contacted David and won his support for our campaign for the Siberian Seven and I felt energized to be connected with old friends.

Our first meeting was in an empty room in the Mermaid Theatre in 2011 where Anthony had been given a rent-free office. Our notebooks were open on a blank page. Anthony outlined his vision and told us, "I want the Human Trafficking Foundation to support and add value to the work of organizations that are doing such good work."

I suggested to Anthony that the Foundation should hold annual awards giving special recognition to people and initiatives that had made an impact. He liked the idea and Bill and I were tasked with organizing the first awards events (for the media), in the House of Lords, which David Alton hosted in 2011 – on Anti-Slavery Day.

We received further encouragement from the Prime Minister who held a reception at Downing Street that same year to signal his approval of Anti-Slavery Day. We crammed into one of the ornate reception rooms to be welcomed by Mr Cameron, who declared, "I'm delighted that so many organizations have taken up the fight against modern slavery. This is an important issue and a priority for this government." Undoubtedly, the NGOs (including us) at Downing Street would be monitoring his words in the months ahead; still, it was good to hear a Prime Minister speak up in this way.

Bill and I left Downing Street early. To promote Anti-Slavery Day we joined with other organizations to launch "Dangerous Songs that Changed the World", to show how the music of the African slaves in America had influenced modern popular music.

We held the meeting at Holy Trinity Clapham in South London, the church attended by Wilberforce that became the nerve centre for the abolitionist movement. David Alton launched the landmark event from the pulpit used by John Newton, the slave trader turned preacher who wrote "Amazing Grace". I always thought of David as a twenty-first-century Wilberforce, and there was something particularly moving about hearing him speak about modern slavery from that historically significant location. It was also stirring to see Hazel Thompson's series of images from her investigation for The Body Shop's campaign into trafficking in South Africa before the World Cup in 2010.

The Human Trafficking Foundation seemed to fill a gap, as over time about fifty organizations joined the network and several important initiatives emerged. In times such as these, I recognized the value of strength in numbers. The issue of trafficking was beyond the scope of any single group and needed a coalition such as this to join forces to act against modern slavery. Anthony had the vision to make it a reality and we believed that linking with others would strengthen our struggle against injustice.

There is no single strategy that will end the phenomenon of trafficking. In the past, the state was the main actor in the theatre of abuse against vulnerable and exploited people. Now criminals and smaller pockets of groups, sometimes individuals, have stolen the lead. It's not difficult to understand why human trafficking has proved popular. There are low start-up costs, minimal risks, high profits, and increasing demand. Criminals prefer trafficking people over drugs and arms for one simple reason: they can be sold time and again.

With the population exploding, human trafficking is destined to be a defining issue of the twenty-first century. While slavery was never fully abolished, change has come with a fresh awareness that slavery is wrong. This has been accompanied by a determination and a renewed sense of purpose that we can and must act to end it.

That's the first step of an important journey.

CHAPTER 17

Sacrifice

Raising Awareness of Modern-Day Child Sacrifice,
2010–present

I read the story in London's *Evening Standard* with horror and revulsion that gave way to an abiding sadness. In September, 2001, the torso of a small child had been discovered in the Thames near London's Tower Bridge. The boy's head, arms, and legs were missing and the body had been drained of its blood. Commander Andy Baker told the press, "Until we can identify him and his family, we will act as his family." The police named him Adam.

The detectives had little to go on. The boy was wearing orange shorts. After investigating, the police learned that only Woolworth's stores in Germany and Austria sold such clothes. Pioneering scientific techniques traced properties in Adam's bones to his native country of Nigeria. Forensic examination of his intestine by plant experts at Kew Gardens pointed to an area near Benin City.

Adam's body was discovered with the gift of time. Perhaps just one more tide, one more rolling of the waves, and the torso would have been swept into the North Sea. And no one would have known that Adam had walked the earth. But despite dogged work by detectives, some clues, a few suspects, and the disclosure of the boy's real name, Ikpomwosa (by ITV's Ronke Phillips) – Adam remained the only unsolved child murder case in London.

The manner of the dismemberment convinced the police that Adam was the victim of a ritualistic juju murder by someone who believed they could gain power from this act of witchcraft. It seemed incredible that the crime of child sacrifice could occur in the heart of Britain's capital city in the twenty-first century. It was equally astonishing to learn that this was not an isolated case. I couldn't imagine who would practice this juju crime of witchcraft, and I was unprepared for what I would discover as I investigated further.

The victims

In April 2010, a young filmmaker, Kirsty Jones, introduced me to Peter Sewakiryanga from Kyampisi in Uganda. He was a dedicated young pastor who had a chilling story to tell the world. As Peter uncovered the mysterious, bizarre, nightmarish world of witchcraft murders, I was struck by the similarities to London's unsolved shocking torso murder. Peter told me of a young boy in his care.

Allan Ssembatya was kidnapped on his way home from school on 19 October 2009 in Mukono, a village about 30 kilometres east of Kampala. His kidnappers took the seven-year-old boy to a witchdoctor's shrine. What happened next was hard to describe because of its savage barbarism. Allan was cut, mutilated, and castrated. He was struck in the head with a machete and his skull was sliced open. Allan was dumped in a bush near his village home where he was found unconscious in a pool of blood. He was rushed to hospital and was in a coma for a month. Over time, Allan made a remarkable recovery, despite a weakness in the left side of his body. In Uganda, he was called the "miracle child".

Allan's father, Hudson Semwanga, worked as a barber and operated his own hair-cutting business from the roadside. He sold the stall to care for his son, and earned money as a labourer on building sites to pay for his son's treatment and to provide food for his family.

Peter knew the identity of Allan's three abductors: a witchdoctor named Awali, his brother Abass, and a man named Paul. The information was handed to the police with a case still pending. But there were many cases pending, backlogged in the courts.

The government's task force set up to investigate child sacrifice reported fourteen ritual child murders in 2010, but police figures were based on "conclusive investigations". Peter told us there were more victims in his parish than official statistics for the entire country. Most cases weren't reported; people know the police won't come. When Peter called the police he paid the petrol for the vehicle to be sure they turned up. Everyone agreed on one thing: the numbers were high, and rising. About 3,000 children went missing annually, many thought to have been murdered in witchcraft ceremonies. In May 2010, the *Weekly Message News* reported, "Over 900 children feared sacrificed or trafficked."

Human sacrifice was an ancient juju (black magic/witchcraft) ritual but its revival in recent years has puzzled many Ugandans as it was not part of traditional culture in Uganda. To some, child sacrifice is a criminal activity undertaken by a corrupt underworld posing as traditional healers with the intention of exploiting people's religious beliefs and superstitions in order to profit financially. Uganda's flourishing economy has seen the country's rich and privileged turn to witchcraft, paying vast sums of money to witchdoctors in the belief that such magic rituals using blood and body parts would increase their wealth and power. Children are considered a commodity of exchange and child sacrifice has become a commercial business.

* * *

Thirteen-year-old Joseph Kasirye was abducted from his home in Kayuggi village in the Masaka District on 27 October 2008; a few days later, his decomposing, headless corpse was found in a swamp. All the blood had been drained from his body and it was evident that the child had been killed in a ritual sacrifice.

The murder of Joseph and the subsequent trial created a sensation in Uganda and is remembered as the most high-profile case of its kind. The trial started in August 2009 in the High Court at Masaka and the prime suspect in the case was Godfrey Kato Kajubi, a prominent businessman with an extensive property portfolio with real estate in Uganda, and allegedly in the UK.

Kajubi was accused of paying a witchdoctor, Umar Kateregga, and his Tanzanian wife, Mariam Nabukeera, to behead Joseph in October 2008 for a witchcraft ritual. The business tycoon allegedly promised the couple 12 million Ugandan shillings (£2,626) but had only paid them 380,000 Ugandan shillings (£83). He guaranteed them the balance of the money after they produced an additional three human heads, but they were arrested before they could complete their macabre assignment.

The court heard that tyre tracks from Kajubi's car were found at the home of Kateregga, and mobile phone records showed that Kajubi had telephoned the witchdoctor on the night of the murder. The court heard from twenty-two witnesses, and in November 2008, *New Vision* reported, "The police said Joseph's body parts were buried in a city mansion which Kajubi is constructing."

In a dramatic twist, the court dropped charges against the witchdoctor and his wife when they turned state witnesses. During their evidence, they admitted that they had lured the boy to their home on 27 October, and phoned Kajubi who turned up after midnight with an associate named Stephen. The witchdoctor told the packed courtroom that both Kajubi and Stephen murdered the thirteen-year old boy, cut off his head and genitals, drained the body of all blood, and dumped the torso in a nearby swamp.

Kajubi was found not guilty in April 2010, but the shock verdict was reversed in November. The court of appeal ordered a new murder trial but the businessman disappeared and went on the run. The manhunt ended in December 2011 when he was arrested at a witchdoctor's shrine in a Kampala suburb. In July 2012, Kajubi was sentenced to life imprisonment.

This case provided dramatic evidence that child sacrifice was not confined to rural areas. It was a gruesome criminal practice used by the rich and powerful who turned to ritualistic murder and witchcraft ceremonies for even greater wealth and power.

* * *

In March 2011, George Kabi, a 58-year-old witchdoctor, became the first person to be tried and convicted for the crime of child sacrifice. He was sentenced to fifty years in prison.

Kabi and a gang abducted seven-year-old Roderick Atuhairwe while he was on his way to Masindi Port Primary School in Kiryandongo on 19 July 2010. The witchdoctor tricked the boy with bread laced with chloroform, pretending it had been sent by his father, Patrick Kyamanywa.

Roderick was kidnapped and dragged into a nearby bush where his genitals were cut off. He was found lying in agony in a pool of blood by Alice Nyimijumbi, and the boy was taken to Kiryandongo Hospital.

Outraged neighbours tracked one of the prime suspects to a nearby swamp, where Edward Rugadya, a former student at the school, was found hiding. He was covered in multiple fetishes and amulets. Rugadya tried to escape but was caught and apparently lynched by the mob. Before dying, Rugadya confessed to the crime and named the others involved. Later, Ignatius Tinka, the head of criminal investigations in Masindi, told Uganda Radio Network that Rugadya was being initiated into the witchcraft business. After the incident, seven witchdoctors were arrested.

Roderick picked out George Kabi at an identity parade at Masindi Prison but collapsed immediately afterwards and was unable to continue; two other witchdoctors, Ibrahim Mwandia and Jackson Baguma, suspected to be involved, were released.

Kabi was sentenced to fifty years in prison in 2011, but the boy's mother, Scovia Ayebale, told the newspapers, "I am not satisfied with the sentence (for Kabi), at least I wanted him to get the death sentence."

The witchdoctor was the first person charged under trafficking legislation passed in 2009. There was no law to deal specifically with the crime of child sacrifice.

The witchdoctor speaks

Peter Sewakiryanga and I discussed the complexities of the issue and agreed to work together. We outlined the objectives for our campaign: we would raise awareness, help the survivors, and petition for a new law.

The first support came from within Uganda. The Archbishop of Uganda backed our campaign, along with Wilson Bugembe, an AIDS orphan forced to live off the rubbish dump, and now one of Africa's biggest gospel music stars. A young British musician, Emma Holland, who had worked in Uganda with Peter, wrote "Heal our Land". It was spine-tingling to hear child survivors sing the catchy refrain: "End child sacrifice, and heal our land." We commissioned further research for an in-depth report, and released a short film by the filmmaker who had first approached me about this issue. Wherever we went, the response was the same: shock and disbelief and a promise to help. People signed our petition, watched our DVD, and when we asked friends to "do something amazing" and donate, our supporters were generous and we built Allan and his family a new home away from the scene of his attack.

I was in an Oxfam shop in the spring of 2011 when my BlackBerry rang. It was the television reporter Chris Rogers. He came straight to the point: "I have been following the campaign. I want to make a film for the BBC. Can we work together?"

I knew the impact that a TV programme could make so we set up the filming for the BBC, and in May 2011, Chris and the BBC team went to Uganda. There they met young Allan, the survivor of a sacrificial ritual, and filmed his story.

At Kampala's main hospital, consultant neurosurgeon Michael Muhumuza showed Chris the X-ray scans of Allan's horrific injuries. They revealed missing bone from his skull and damage to the left-hand side of his brain, from the machete that sliced through Allan's head and neck in an attempt to behead him – the work of witchdoctors attempting child sacrifice.

"Allan suffered brain damage, which is common unfortunately; there is not much we can do," explained Dr Muhumuza. "It's quite shocking, I think this is unacceptable, he is just an innocent young child."

One of the tormenting parts of Allan's story was that he could identify his kidnapper, Awali, although the police say they haven't acted because of a lack of evidence. Our partner tracked down Awali and knew that he was still involved with witchcraft ceremonies. Chris and the BBC team went undercover, posing as local businessmen seeking a witchdoctor who could bring prosperity to their construction company. It wasn't long before Awali appeared. He led the undercover journalists into a courtyard behind his home, and to welcome them, he and his helpers wrestled a goat to the ground and slit its throat. "This animal has been sacrificed to bring luck to us all," Awali explained. He then demanded a fee of $390 (£250) for the ritual and asked them to return in a few days.

At the next meeting, Awali invited them into his shrine, which was traditionally built from mud bricks with a straw roof. Inside, the floor was littered with a witchdoctor's tools: herbs, face masks, rattles, and a machete. The witchdoctor explained that this meeting was to discuss the most powerful spell – the sacrifice of a child.

"There are two ways of doing this," he said. "We can bury the child alive on your construction site, or we cut them in different places and put their blood in a bottle of spiritual medicine." Awali grabbed his throat. "If it's a male, the whole head is cut off and his genitals. We will dig a hole at your construction site, and also bury the feet and the hands and put them all together in the hole."

Awali boasted he had sacrificed children many times before and knew what he was doing. After this meeting, the BBC team withdrew from the negotiations.

Later, the TV reporter sat with Allan and his father on the steps of their makeshift house, built from corrugated sheets of metal, while they waited for their new home to be built. Chris told me, "I showed the footage of our meeting with the witchdoctor to Allan on my laptop. He pointed to the screen and said 'Awali!' confirming he is the man who attacked him."

Their notes were handed to the police. Awali is still a free man.

When the BBC saw the results of the filming, they decided to broadcast it over two days, and Chris edited several versions for television and radio. We held our breath.

Chris telephoned on 11 October 2011. He was tired but excited: "It's tomorrow night!"

And it was. The lead on BBC TV News. A documentary on BBC World. Wide radio coverage. This was bold, breakthrough investigative journalism at its best, as an untold, hidden story was exposed to the world. Our report was prominently featured, and Allan won the hearts and minds of viewers everywhere, as they heard his moving story of abduction and escape from sacrifice.

The impact was dramatic and significant. Chris told me later:

> *The documentary was the most downloaded film in the history of the BBC World News channel on its iPlayer service in the UK, US, and Australia. The film and news reports ignited one of the largest ever audience reactions and is one of the most tweeted subjects in the history of the BBC.*

After the broadcast, Lord Alton raised the issue in the House of Lords and Chris Foley MP did the same in the Australian

Parliament. It forced the Ugandan President to admit more needed to be done to tackle child sacrifice and the trafficking of children in Africa and to Europe. At a news conference in October 2011 in Kampala he told reporters, "I will make this my priority."

After the broadcast, we received requests for information and photographs from across the globe. It's not over, but the BBC's film has touched a nerve, and sparked international headlines and debate of this gruesome crime. One year later, in October 2012, the BBC's *Our World* documentary was nominated for an Emmy award, the highest recognition that television can bestow.

The BBC fired a shot of light and it was seen around the world. The best evidence for this was our online petition. The numbers jumped to the thousands as people in over ninety countries (and counting) joined us in demanding a change in the law to bring witchdoctors and traffickers to justice.

CHAPTER 18

What Tomorrow May Bring

The Work That Remains

I sometimes marvel at the footsteps along life's journey that have led me here. In childhood dreams, I saw myself as a cowboy, a boxer, James Dean, Elvis... As an ambitious youth, I romped in the fields of journalism, impressed at the doors that opened with a National Union of Journalists' membership card.

In New York City, one afternoon in the late seventies, I fumbled my way through an interview with my design hero – the legendary Milton Glaser. Glaser has been described as the embodiment of American graphic design and produced some of the most enduring and powerful visual art of our time. His iconic emblem "I 'heart' NY" had been called "the most frequently imitated logo design in human history".

Glaser was gracious to his young fan, generous with his time. When we met, he'd completed an audacious assignment: Glaser had hand drawn the New York skyline onto the glass windows of a circular-shaped restaurant. Standing in the centre of the room gave patrons a panoramic view of that vibrant city, like a window on the world. His inventive idea was located at the restaurant at the top of New York's World Trade Center's Twin Tower.

Glaser chuckled when I asked him where his ideas came from. His instinctive response was, "I don't know where my best ideas come from." Then he mused over the question, and added:

Some ideas come from the objective world, others from the observation of random phenomena. Sometimes, it's the reflection of a neon sign on the sidewalk. It could be the sound of a saxophone in an alley. Creativity comes from the realm of the unknown, from the subconscious. Ideas impose themselves on you whether you want them to or not. The world of the imagination is an artist's passport.

I am known for tearing out obscure snippets from newspapers and stuffing them into files, now several bulging folders. I remain intrigued with ideas and influences and the impact they can have. People will sacrifice a lot – sometimes even themselves – for an idea.

In 2003 I read in *The Wall Street Journal* about a boarding school in Indonesia run by Islamic fundamentalists that had produced many of Indonesia's top terrorist suspects, including alleged participants in the attack on Jakarta's Marriott Hotel and the Bali nightclub bombing in 2002. Dedicated students adhered to a strict code: the school day started with predawn prayers at 3.30 a.m. and ended at 10 p.m. Students were allowed out only once a month, with no more than 10,000 rupiah (about 75p) in their pocket. Anyone who missed any scheduled prayer through the day could get ten strokes of a rattan cane. The slogan over the main classroom building read, "Death in the way of Allah is our highest aspiration". Ideas like this can seize some people's imagination with such savage force that nothing else matters in this earthly life.

I have never considered myself a do-gooder or thought that I would right every wrong but there were a few ideas that drove me on. I wanted to be sure that things changed as a result of the time and resources we used campaigning for children at risk and those suffering injustice. I thought that this idea encapsulated the service and legacy of Jubilee Campaign.

I was also clear that to be effective we should combine practical help with lobbying and have been so inspired by all that David Alton achieved in Parliament. To accomplish this, in 1987 we dedicated Jubilee Campaign as a pressure group, working alongside the charity (Jubilee Action) that we set up five years later.

When it became evident in 2008 that Jubilee Campaign and Jubilee Action would no longer work together, we'd reached a fork in the road: it meant that the trustees of Jubilee Action continued as a separate organization but I played no part.

We registered Jubilee Campaign as a charity (processed in 2009) after Father Shay Cullen, Reverend Devaraj, and others chose to continue their partnership with us to take Jubilee Campaign forward and we began to restructure the organization. In some ways, it was like starting again.

We had the names and addresses of a few people, but supporters who hadn't heard from me got in touch and wanted to know what I was doing and the mailing list grew. I answered every message personally and though this took time, it was heartening to connect directly with some of our supporters again.

The important things in my life

It's not always easy to write about events when you're a player in them, and in writing this book I found myself overdrawn at my memory bank, tangled up with dates while trying to recall activities when many campaigns ran concurrently. I was reminded of moments that left me scorched that are still hard to express in words. Frequently I'd felt like a spectator who received far more than I could give, both humbled and blessed by unfolding events, inspired by those who pulled alongside to lead, encourage, and support.

It's been emotional for me to retrace those early days of Jubilee Campaign. While I provided the strategic vision for the work, it was my family who made the sacrifice, and Joan who struggled with the financial burden of running a home with little money coming in. Joan's faithfulness and courage exceeded my own. While my vision was both noble and global, I had obscured the needs of those nearest to me. I was MIA (missing in action) at home for lots of the time. I wasn't there and I didn't know it. Joan had been the anchor, the rock, putting us first, sacrificing her dreams, her career, for us – her family – and doing it instinctively, joyfully; such dedication didn't seek a reward but deserved recognition. It was love beyond understanding or expectation, something to treasure and emulate.

With the passage of time, I discerned that the important things in my life were my faith and my family: Joan, Rachel, Luke – and Jessica. Seth and Eden made Rachel's childhood dream come true as she got to play house for real with Matt. Luke put his techno-savvy skills to work to develop the campaign online and gave direction to the changes in this book with his gift for timing and language, all this amid discovering – with Holly – the surprise and joy of parenthood with the arrival of Lily Grace.

Jubilee Campaign gave me a mission, while my family brought meaning to my life, and from this sustaining relationship has come a sense of belonging.

My beloved Jessica

I awoke on the morning of 27 December 2007 with a darkness in myself, a sense of foreboding, something I can't explain. I thought I'd kept my feelings hidden, buried deep within. Our friends, Janet and Craig Rickards, dropped in unexpectedly late morning to borrow something. They left puzzled over why I seemed upset, and wondered if they had annoyed me.

I had a premonition over that Christmas season, and on that day, the worst day of my life, it came true. Soon after Craig and Janet had left, we discovered that Jessica had passed in the night...

The shock of losing my beloved daughter Jessica, aged just twenty-two years, has been like an earthquake in my heart and life. Jessica and I were exceptionally close and went on many adventures together. From an early age, Jess enjoyed being part of the Jubilee team. She spent her holidays in the office as our youngest recruit and took an active part in many campaigns. Jessica travelled to India with me, became a "sister" to Asha, and had plans to return. Reverend Devaraj treated her like his own daughter, and earlier in 2007, when she was troubled, he telephoned her from Mumbai encouraging her to visit. Jessica was amazed by the timing of his call and telephoned me immediately afterwards: "Dad! Reverend Devaraj phoned me. Guess what? I was in the midst of talking to my friends about him and the work when he called. I was telling everyone that I wanted to go to back to India and work with him."

She had already talked to Father Shay about visiting the Philippines as a volunteer at Preda, and had made an appointment with Hazel Thompson to discuss an investigation in Zimbabwe. Jess had gone to Africa in April 2004 and was moved by the beauty of the country but troubled by the poverty and injustice she witnessed. She asked me if Hazel would help and told me, "I really want her to get involved. I want her to go to Zimbabwe."

Jessica's passing was ruled an accidental death. I was spared the sensation of rage, the pointless fury that causes us to shake our fist at God and others. Perhaps it was the "panic of loss" that seized me, the raging grief that had encompassed all I could see and feel. The days that passed didn't bring comfort and I didn't find time a healer.

George Verwer, now retired from OM, stored over a hundred photo albums in a cabinet in his cramped office in their family home in West Wickham, Kent. The albums held photographs of people he knew from all over the world and served as a reminder to communicate and pray for them. George noticed that an album was separated from the others and had got stuck behind a bookcase. He reached out for the lost album and with some difficulty retrieved it by knocking it out with a ruler. The album slid out and fell on the floor. It flipped open to a page with a photo of Jessica.

George took it to his wife Drena and said, "Look, that's Jessica." He then took the album to its rightful place on the shelf. It was home.

This happened a few days after Jessica passed. I drew solace from the symbolism of this incident. In my heart, I felt Jessica was at peace, at home.

We decided to set up charitable tributes in Jessica's memory to complete her unfulfilled dreams to help vulnerable children, and when George heard this he handed us a cheque for £1,000. This first donation was followed by many, including a personal gift of 3,000 euros by Father Shay to start the Jessica Smith Scholarship Fund, a programme that he set up to provide opportunities for trafficked, exploited, and underprivileged children in the Philippines who can't afford further education.

He was confident that lives would be transformed by this simple but effective idea, and sent me this message:

> *It seems only yesterday that we were there together. That last meal together is frozen in time for me. This is a beautiful way to remember Jessie, something that will live on and on... giving new life to the impoverished is best done this way, as whole lives, families, and generations are best influenced through education, especially for young girls.*

Shay wrote an article to promote the programme and reported that it was doing well with no drop-outs. He told me, "Yes, I look on them as Jessica's Kids. This is what she would have been doing. Working in the developing world. Giving life into the future for kids that would otherwise end up on the dumpsite of humanity. Now they have a bright future – and their children also."

We chose countries where Jess had visited or planned to visit (the Philippines, India, and Zimbabwe), but I didn't find it easy to work on these tributes so I was grateful to friends who stepped up to help. Linda Denne ran the Virgin London Marathon in 2011 to raise funds and awareness for "Jessica's House", a programme that we wanted to start to help AIDS orphans in Zimbabwe, and Jessie's friend Mrs Bernadette Charehwa offered to help with contacts inside the country.

Our supporters were generous, and I was touched at the number of people who reached out to me. Some shared personal details of their own loss; others sent heartfelt messages of consolation – cards, letters, poems, books. I treasured each one.

Joan and I have grown closer during this winter season. I have found myself drawn to seek God in a new way. Still, I don't think I will ever get over this indescribable loss and Jessica's sudden passing.

I felt my life change when I held Jessica in my arms minutes after she was born. Now my life has changed again because I can no longer feel her touch or hold her in my arms.

I read that in the game of chess, every move we make changes the way the world exists. And that's how it has been for me. I live in a world that still chugs along with people going about their affairs but for me the world has changed. I can't go back to how things were and I have to find a way to live amid the way the world exists now.

I still cannot imagine what life will be like without Jessica by my side. I think of her every day, and every step has a memory. I see her face when I turn, feel her spirit with every movement of the earth. I still have that sense of an earthquake in my heart...

Healing power of music

I've always been stirred by music. My grandmother was a musician, as was my mother, and as a child our home was filled with the latest rhythms. But since Jessica's passing, I haven't been able to listen to any of the music that I used to play. The only time this music is heard these days is when Luke is in the car, and he'll bring a handful of CDs, many that he's snaffled from me.

I was drawn out of my emotional deep freeze by Samuel Barber's *Adagio for Strings*. The rich, powerful music stirred something within. Later, the thawing continued with music inspired by the slaves of Africa – mainly gospel and spirituals – as the songs reached out from the past and drew me in. I was moved by their pain and anguish expressed – no, invested – in music as a legacy of their experience. The slaves in America were captured spirits torn from their home and family, adrift and tormented in a foreign land. And from this dark, brooding terrain would rise a music that would influence and change the musical landscape forever.

I drew comfort from that great freedom hymn by James Cleveland, and played it repeatedly:

> *I don't feel no ways tired*
> *I've come too far from where I started from*
> *Nobody told me that the road would be easy*
> *I don't believe He brought me this far to leave me*

Everything I thought and believed was captured in this soaring music, and it lifted me.

My friend Bill Hampson introduced me to the gospel star Jessy Dixon, who recorded and toured with Paul Simon for seven years. In 2009 Bill asked me to meet Jessy's flight at Heathrow and drive him to a gig in Birmingham. He was jet-lagged after a gruelling journey with delays and missed connections but the road to Birmingham was marked by tales of music and missed turns. Jessy's gift to us has been one more glorious song that I carry with me these days as an anthem of personal inspiration:

> *We still have work*
> *We still have work*

We still have work to do
Until the sun shines down
On more than just a few
We still have work to do

After the trauma of losing Jessica, I didn't know if there was still a place for me and any "work to do" or if any strength remained after being bowed down with the exhaustion of the grieving process.

Health scare

Starting around 2011, my health took a hit. I contracted various ailments but the National Health Service were brilliant and put me through several tests. Joan was on the case and detected another threat in late 2011. My blood-sugar levels were high, and though my weight was never an issue, I had recently acquired a spare tyre around my middle. Joan predicted that I would be diagnosed with type 2 diabetes and in January 2012 this was confirmed. Stress was most likely the cause and I couldn't argue with that. On the day of the diagnosis, I walked out of the health clinic with a prescription for a drug that I would be required to take for the rest of my life, leading on to regular injections for insulin.

Joan had already embarked on a crash course into responses to diabetes, and her day and night research produced several options for us to consider. We settled on Dr Calvin Ezrin, an endocrinologist, and followed the dietary advice set out in his book *The Type 2 Diabetes Diet Book*. It was tough but I had set my mind on the first and only diet I have ever been on, and had surprisingly few cravings and no secret chocolate binges.

Alongside this we spent half an hour every day on a brisk walk. At first, I tested my blood sugar after every meal, but as it was low, I never took the drugs. Joan supported me and followed the diet with me. When I returned to the health clinic after three months, my blood-sugar readings were normal, and they told me that this was the most dramatic result they had seen.

I came off Dr Ezrin's extreme diet having evolved new taste buds. I acquired an appetite for green tea, fish, vegetables, nuts, fruit, and dark chocolate. I didn't know if I could keep up this new food lifestyle but followed a menu low in carbohydrates, high in vegetables, and rich in olive oil, similar to a Mediterranean diet, and gradually added a more normal selection of food. One year later, when I attended my annual check-up, in February 2013, the diagnosis was that my diabetes had been reversed, and the disease was now controlled by diet and exercise.

These days, I have the freedom to eat anything (and frequently do) but I try to choose wisely. Joan still has the drug prescription that I was originally given as a reminder of how different things could have been.

More to do

I can't see far down the road. I know there are meetings and plans and "work to do".

With friends who can help with the Jessica Smith Scholarship Fund set up by Father Shay in the Philippines, and the other tributes for Jessica in India and Zimbabwe.

With Hazel Thompson. After exciting meetings at Apple's London office, senior figures in the organization were captivated by Hazel's searing images exposing trafficking and modern slavery in India. As a result, they agreed to back the creation of an Apple iBook and gave Hazel unprecedented support. It was a breakthrough moment. Hazel's digital multimedia interactive iBook will carry images, video, text, and maps and will be sold on iTunes – available online worldwide – with all the profits from the sale going through Jubilee Campaign to support Bombay Teen Challenge's rescue mission for orphaned and abandoned children from Mumbai's red light district. Hazel is a visionary and it's been exhilarating to be a part of such an amazing project.

With Sarah de Carvalho from Happy Child. Sarah has great contacts and boundless energy and asked me to develop a campaign with her to fight child trafficking and sex tourism during the World Cup in Brazil (in 2014). Our "It's a Penalty" campaign has already gained support from Chelsea footballers, CEOP (Child Exploitation and Online Protection Centre/National Crime Agency), and other key players.

With Bill Hampson. After all these years, it was as though nothing had changed, as we sat together to explore ways to make Anti-Slavery Day a landmark in the national calendar and plotted further escapades.

With my son Luke, who has put his knowledge of algorithms, advanced mathematics, and calculus to work, and taken on the assignment to create an app for our campaigns.

There are moments in life when we are called to redefine ourselves. Trouble and strife, tests and challenges are difficult and come to us all. Destructive, distressing, destabilizing... but over time, we understand that such things define and mould and illuminate our character. It is exactly at such moments that the depths of relationships, commitments, and faith are anchored.

Some things have changed for sure, but that passion for justice hasn't been extinguished – it still flickers. These days my mission seems to be to inspire other people to have a mission. My faith and spiritual journey remains a work-in-progress but I still cling to all that I believe in, difficult as that can be sometimes. I feel the same way about our mission as I did when Joan and I were writing appeals and campaign petitions on second-hand IBM Selectric "golfball" typewriters – today, it's emails and Facebook and apps and websites and wi-fi and VoIP and Google. And every now and then, I hear Jessy Dixon's distinctive voice calling out, "We still have work..."

Get in touch with Danny Smith
danny@jubileecampaign.co.uk

Find out more about Jubilee Campaign

Jubilee Campaign
PO Box 700
Addlestone
Surrey KT15 9BW
United Kingdom

www.jubileecampaign.co.uk

"Jubilee Campaign" on Facebook